"Sermons By Pickup"

This series was delivered in the church building at Clearwater, Florida February 25 through March 6, 1952. They were recorded and written here just as delivered.

edited by

H.E. Phillips

Truth
Publications

Taking His hand,
Helping each other home.
TM

ISBN 10: 1-58427-163-9

ISBN 13: 978-158427-163-5

First Printing: 2006

Truth Publications, Inc.
CEI Bookstore
220 S. Marion St., Athens, AL 35611
855-492-6657
sales@truthpublications.com
www.truthbooks.com

HARRY WILSON PICKUP, SR.

To my beloved companion, Libby, the great-est preacher's wife I have ever known—who has joyfully shared the years of sunshine and sorrow as helper, advisor and faithful co-worker—this volume is affectionately ded-icated.

HARRY PICKUP.

INTRODUCTION

The preparations were made early in 1952 to record and put in permanent form a series of sermons by Harry Pickup. Many who knew of these plans insisted that it be done and that a copy of the book be reserved for them.

Harry Wilson Pickup, the author of this book, was born August 9th, 1900 in Brooklyn, New York. He was the fourth son of George Alexander and Myra Rebecca Pickup. When Harry was still a small child his father moved to Nashville, Tennessee where he operated his own business as a manufacturer of rubber printing specialties. Harry Pickup attended school at Nashville and later worked with his father for a number of years.

His father was not a religious man, in the usual manner of speaking, although holding before his children a high standard of morality and decency. His mother was not a member of any religious body, although having somewhat more of a religious inclination than his father. Often in later years Brother Pickup tried to talk to them about the Bible but with no success. He has one sister who is a member of the church of the Lord.

Early in life Harry Pickup displayed his religious tendencies. With his oldest brother, he attended the Baptist Church and Sunday School for a number of years. But due to his association with young people in the church of Christ, he later began to attend there and went regularly for several years. The sermons of brethren J. E. Acuff, Grant, Herbert Winkler, G. W. Sweeney and some others did much to bring him to a knowledge of the truth.

Harry was baptized into Christ by J. E. Acuff on one Sunday night in August, 1918, after he had walked down the aisle on the old Charlotte Avenue church building in Nashville, Tennessee that Sunday morning. From that hour when he was baptized into "our Lord and Saviour Jesus Christ" he has spent many years in a glorious service in the Kingdom of Christ.

On March 9, 1922 Harry Pickup was united in marriage to Miss Margaret Elizabeth Heist of Nashville, Tennessee, and for 30 years she has been his faithful and helpful companion. To them God has given a boy and a girl: Harry, Jr. who is now preaching the gospel of Christ in Phoenix, Arizona, and Jeanne, Mrs. John A. Zellner, who lives in Floral City, Florida.

The gospel preacher who deserves the credit for starting Brother Pickup on the road to preaching the gospel is William Allan Cameron of St. Petersburg, Florida. Brother Cameron has been preaching the gospel for nearly 60 years, most of which have been spent in Florida. In January, 1925 Brother Pickup went to St. Petersburg because of his health. He began attending the Ninth Street church of Christ. (The church was then located on Ninth Street, long before the new and larger building was built on the present location). There he came in contact with Brother Cameron, who saw in Harry the ability to do public work in the church, and as Brother Cameron reports: "Without asking Harry before hand, I just said to the congregation one Wednesday night, 'Next Wednesday night Harry Pickup will speak to us on the subject: *Abraham, His Life and Times.*' As soon as the service was over Harry came to me and said, 'I can't do that; I never stood before an audience in my life.' I told him to get ready and I would help him. The next Wednesday night he gave a good lesson on the subject I had assigned to him. Since that time he has been preaching the gospel of Christ." That was in March, 1925. When he moved back to Nashville, he was given a class of young people at the Charlotte Avenue church of Christ, and he made such a success with that class that he was encouraged to do some preaching and teaching at other places. The ones who were active in his early training were those responsible for his becoming a Christian.

In July, 1926 he began his successful career of gospel preaching at the Tennessee State Prison at Nashville. He continued this for about three years, (as he has often said: "I was in the pen for three years,") during which time he preached for different congregations in the Nashville area and in Davidson county. For a number of years he worked with his father in the daytime and preached in meetings around Nashville at night. He drove a Model T Ford as far as 25 and 30 miles in these meetings.

His first full time work as a preacher was with the Park Avenue church of Christ in LaGrange, Ga. in 1934. He was with this congregation for four years. He then moved to the University Avenue church of Christ in Gainesville, Florida where he labored for three years. From Gainesville he moved to the church in Arlington, Va. where he stayed for six years. For the past three years he has been with the Howard Avenue church of Christ in Tampa, Florida and is also an instructor at Florida Christian College.

Brother Pickup has preached in meetings and local work in Florida, Alabama, Georgia, Mississippi, Tennessee, North Carolina, Virginia, Pennsylvania, Maryland, New Jersey, New York, Indiana, Kentucky, Illinois, Arkansas and Texas.

I have known Harry Pickup for a number of years as a preacher, a man, a friend and brother. I know of no man in whom I have more confidence and personal interest than Harry Pickup. His sincerity is unsurpassed; his love for the truth is the purest; his uncompromising disposition is outstanding; his compassion and love for lost souls is of the greatest; his humility is most like Christ; his convictions are deep; his examples of Christianity are of the best.

With profit I have counseled him on many occasions, and never has he been too busy to help. I am glad to see some of his sermons embalmed and preserved in print for the future generations to read after his tongue lies silent in the grave. These sermons are given in his own inimitable style just as he delivered them, with but few changes to make better reading. My prayer is that this book will be instrumental in leading souls to Christ, in bringing Christians back to the Lord and in building up the church in the knowledge of Christ. I am certain that this is also the sole desire of the author, Harry Pickup.

H. E. PHILLIPS.

CONTENTS

THE BATTLE-GROUNDS OF THOSE WHO BUILD

H. E. PHILLIPS: We appreciate very much the presence of this number tonight for the beginning service in this series of meetings. We are grateful for a number who have come from other congregations in this county to be here with us in this opening night. I am sure that others would have been here had the weather been a little better than it is.

Tonight Brother Pickup is to begin this series on the subject: *The Battleground Of Those Who Build.* I want to suggest in the very beginning that everyone do the very best that he can to advertise these meetings and the sermon subjects each evening. We can do a great deal to encourage those of our acquaintances and our friends and neighbors to come to these services if we will advertise them.

One other thing I want to say before we begin the service tonight: Each of us ought to engage to the best of our ability in the singing of these hymns of praise. We ought to sing them to worship God; to admonish, to edify and encourage others. Everyone, if you can sing at all, ought to join in these songs for that reason. It is a lot better for the one who is trying to direct the singing, and, of course, it is much better for the one who is trying to preach the gospel. Before we begin to sing these songs, we are going to ask Brother Lloyd Farless to lead us in a word of prayer.

(Prayer directed by Brother Farless)

PHILLIPS: Most of you, especially of this congregation and vicinity, know Brother Harry Pickup. You know his good wife also. We are happy tonight to have both of them with us in this series of efforts, beginning his part tonight in preaching the gospel of Christ. I say this humbly—I do not want to think more of any man that I ought to think—but there are some men who stand above others in our estimation and judgment as a gospel preacher. In

1

my judgment Harry Pickup is a man who, as a gospel
preacher, is about as good as I have ever heard or known.
Perhaps that is because I know him better as a man than
I do some of the others.   He is capable from the stand-
point of the knowledge of the Scriptures to preach the
Word of God, and he is able so far as ability is concerned
by natural endowment.   It is good for us I think—good
for the church—to have him with us in this series of efforts.
As I tried to point out last evening in some remarks that
I made regarding our responsibilities in this series of efforts and the opportunities that are open beginning tonight
to save the souls of men and women, rests not on his shoulders alone but upon the shoulders of everyone of us.   We
ought to do our part.   I am sure he will do his part, at least
that is the confidence that I have in him, and I'm sure
that the elders of this congregation have the same confidence in him.

We want to invite you who are our neighbors in this
community and those of neighboring congregations to visit
with us as often as you can.   I would suggest that you bring
along your Bibles and engage in a careful study with us
as we go along from night to night, or else bring paper
and pencil and write down the Scriptures that are given
and go home and investigate to see whether or not these
things are so.   I'm sure if you will do that, you will come
back again and again, and before this series of efforts shall
end you will obey the gospel.

We have some visitors tonight from Largo, from Dune-
din, from Tarpon Springs and perhaps other places.   Among
them Brother Leon Humphries, my brother and friend from
Largo, and we are going to ask him at this time to lead us
while we pray.   After this prayer and the singing of the
next song—"Rock of Ages"—Brother Pickup will bring us
the lesson for the evening.   Let us stand while we pray,
and remain standing for the song.

PICKUP: I want to assure you, friends, in the very
beginning of this meeting, that the many kind things that
Brother Phillips expressed concerning me is mutual with

regard to my feeling for him. I appreciate the fine work that he has been doing for a long, long time. I have looked forward with great joy to working with him and you of this congregation in this meeting that we are now beginning this evening. I want you to know that I will do my best to preach the gospel of Christ in its purity and simplicity, to try to edify the church and build up the Cause by leading men and women, who do not know the truth, to understand better the things that God would have them to know about the Bible and about themselves.

I want to try tonight to lay a foundation, or ground work, for this meeting, and I can think of nothing better than to begin by reading a few passages of Scripture from Paul's second letter to his young son in the gospel, Timothy, the fourth chapter, beginning at verse one. He says: "I charge thee therefore before God, and the Lord Jesus Christ, who shall judge the quick and the dead at His appearing and His kingdom; preach the word; be instant in season, out of season; reprove, rebuke, exhort with all longsuffering and doctrine. For the time will come when they will not endure sound doctrine; but after their own lusts shall they heap to themselves teachers, having itching ears; and they shall turn away their ears from the truth, and shall be turned unto fables. But watch thou in all things, endure afflictions, do the work of an evangelist, make full proof of thy ministry. For I am now ready to be offered, and the time of my departure is at hand. I have fought a good fight, I have finished my course, I have kept the faith: henceforth there is laid up for me a crown of righteousness, which the Lord, the righteous judge, shall give me at that day: and not to me only, but unto all them also that love His appearing."

There are numerous statements in that passage that we could well comment upon but I have in mind tonight one major idea; that is the statement that Paul uses in which he mentions the fight of faith. In other words, we are speaking tonight about "The Battle-grounds of Those Who Build;" building on the foundation that God would have us to build upon, or putting it in the way that we have expressed it in our sermon topic: the place where we have to fight as we build the Kingdom of God.

You know, from the very beginning of time man has had a conflict on his hands. It has been necessary for him to fight the foes that were presented to him by Satan, and where ever he has gone on the face of the earth, from the time that he lost the first battle in the garden of Eden until the last man who shall live upon this earth, man's every life is fraught with the responsibility of waging a warfare. I think we need to know that, and we need to instruct people that when they become members of the body of Christ they are going to have to fight, and, fight on these various battlegrounds. There is not just one ground upon which people fight, my friends, but many. The older that you grow in the service of your Lord the more you come to realize that. Those of us who have been in the church for a number of years have come to appreciate the fact that these things are true. Now without spending any time in thinking about the conditions of man today, but rather getting directly to our subject, I want you to notice some of the passages of Scripture that we call to your attention in getting you to understand and appreciate the very thing that we are trying to present to you tonight. You know, I spend considerable time, usually, in my introductions, and those of you who have heard me preach much, know that I think it is profitable to spend that time. For instance, if we can get a sermon properly introduced, it doesn't take so long to draw the conclusions and to wind up the whole affair. I want you tonight to see with me some of the basic ideas that we are going to talk about, and then we will use a few examples and the sermon will be over.

First of all I want you to notice that in the life of the Lord Jesus Christ he had to wage a warfare. Why, he had not been engaged in his public ministry very long until he turned over the tables of the money changers and drove the wicked people out of the temple. Almost the last act that he performed was a similar act. He drove out the money changers near the end of His public ministry, and said, "You have made my Father's house a house of merchandise."

I'm looking at a passage in I Timothy 6:12 where Paul told Timothy: "Fight the good fight of faith, lay hold on the life eternal, whereunto thou wast called, and didst confess the good confession in the sight of many witnesses." Thus we see that Paul expresses the idea of conflict. And I think we need to know that today. I can think of nothing better than to inform the people that actually we are not shadow boxing, but we are engaged in a real conflict against the forces of evil. It was Paul who also said, as we read for you just a few moments ago: "I have fought a good fight, I have finished my course, I have kept the faith." Now the whole idea was built upon his conflict with satan, and wherever he went he found the forces of evil before him, and the same groups that his Lord had to fight when on earth, Paul found himself in conflict with those same forces of evil. That's also true in the Old Testament, and it's really to the Old Testament tonight that we go for our major example as we look at the battle-grounds of faith. We could say that Jesus is an example of fighting upon these battle grounds. So is Paul, and so is Peter, but I think we have one concrete illustration in the Old Testament, in the book of Nehemiah, that I want to use as my illustration tonight in *The Battle-Grounds of Those Who Build*.

First, I want to remind you of the fact that Nehemiah wanted to go back and build again the city of Jerusalem. You remember how that Nehemiah was concerned very much about this as he went about the business of serving the king. He was concerned about the walls of the city that had fallen down. You remember the people of Israel had been taken into captivity, and the city of Jerusalem at that time was lying in waste, and all the time that Nehemiah was about the duties of serving the king, and he was a favorite of the king, he was thinking about his beloved city. He said to himself, "I'd like to go back and build the

walls of my home city, my native town." The king understood one day, that something was wrong with Nehemiah.
He asked him about it, and as a result they went back to
the city and began to build.

Now friends, when people begin to build, they get in
trouble, that is, there are forces of evil about them that try
to offset the building that is done, and, if possible, to prevent the building up of that which might be according to
the ways of God. So, Nehemiah and the people of Israel,
as they went back and started to rebuild the city of Jerusalem, serve as the illustration that I want to call to your
attention tonight on the various battle-grounds that they
had to fight upon. You can immediately see the reference
that I'm making to this matter, and that the application I'm
making to the incident is, that you too will have to fight
upon those same battle-grounds.

Now here is the first one that I want you to notice. In
the 4th chapter of the book of Nehemiah, and beginning
with verse 1, through verse 3, and then reading the 6th
verse, I want you to notice what the record says. "It came
to pass, that when Sanballat heard that we builded the
wall, he was wroth, and took great indignation, and mocked
the Jews. And he spake before his brethren and the army
of Samaria, and said, What do these feeble Jews? will
they fortify themselves? will they sacrifice? will they make
an end in a day? will they revive the stones out of the
heaps of the rubbish which are burned? Now Tobiah the
Ammonite was by him, and he said, Even that which they
build, if a fox go up, he shall even break down their stone
wall."

My first point this evening, and the first battle-ground,
I think, is the battle-ground of ridicule and criticism. These
people said, as these men went about the business of building, "You can't build the walls; you are not strong enough
to build this wall of the city of Jerusalem." Thus they
attempted by every means known to them, by even suggesting that the thing was so weak and their efforts were
so feeble that if a fox, a little animal, should go up against

the wall, the thing would fall down. Thus, we see that these people of God through ridicule and criticism were presented with one of the first of their battles that they had to fight. I want you to see how they answered that challenge. In verse 6 it says: "So we build the wall; and all the wall was joined together unto the half thereof: for the people had a mind to work." You know, one of the best ways in the world to fight the enemy of criticism is to get the job done. One of the best ways in the world to demonstrate the desire and power to do the work of the Lord is to do it. The individual who has the ability, the understanding, the knowledge, the wherewith, so to speak, and doesn't do it, is but succumbing to the power of criticism and ridicule that many times breaks down some of the strongest. I want to suggest, therefore, my friends, as you build the cause of Christ in this community, as you build up the work of the Lord, as you are attempting to do, and as you have been doing, one of the things that you are going to have to constantly fight is to fight ridicule and criticism. It is a common battle ground today; and today we must overcome the enemy on that battle ground the same as did others that we read about in the Bible.

I have the Bible open at the 14th chapter of the book of Acts—the New Testament—and I want you to see that when Paul was preaching in Iconium he had the same problem to contend with. Listen to verse 2: "But the unbelieving Jews stirred up the Gentiles, and made their minds evil affected against the brethren." There is the turning of the minds of the people against the brethren of Paul. By criticism, and by the means that they employed in that procedure, we see the church is weakened because of the efforts that are put forth here. Sometimes individuals are affected by this to the extent that they say, "Well, I might as well give up." I have even known people to quit the church because they couldn't take the criticism from, sometimes, members of their own families, sometimes from friends, sometimes from business associates. They say: "Well, it does look like we ought to be bigger than we are. It does look like we ought to be more significant than we are." But do you know friends, it doesn't necessarily follow that because a thing is large or small that it is right? That isn't the standard by which God judges things. If you are going to allow criticism and ridicule to prevent you from doing the Lord's will, then you are losing the first battle that you have to fight in the kingdom of your Lord.

But I want you to notice still another statement that we find here as I turn again to the Old Testament and read from the book of Nehemiah concerning the second of these battle grounds. In the 14th verse of the 4th chapter of Nehemiah, the record says: "And I looked, and rose up, and said unto the nobles, and to the rulers, and to the rest of the people, Be not ye afraid of them: remember the Lord, which is great and terrible, and fight for your brethren, your sons, and your daughters, your wives, and your houses." Back in the 8th verse he says: "And conspired all of them together to come and to fight against Jerusalem, and to hinder it." The result of it is that they said, "Well, all right, fellows, if that's the way you want it, that's the way it will be."

You know, I like that spirit. I like the fact that, although these Jews, feeble in the minds of the people, had very little with which to fight, they said, "Well, we are going to do the best we can. We are going out and we are going to meet the enemy on the battle field, if need be." Do you know how much preparation they made? As they built with one hand they held the sword in the other. They were not only building, but they were ready to fight. They were anxious to do the Lord's work, and be not hindered by these enemies if possible, but they said, "If that's the way you want it, all right, we'll meet you out there on the battle field." But you know they did not have to wager any major warfare or any major battles because as soon as the enemy saw that these men intended to do what they had set their hands to do, the enemy backed down.

I want to tell you, friends, I believe that is the thing we have to do today. I don't mean that we have to go around with a chip on our shoulder and say, "Knock it off!" I remember when I first started preaching, I didn't know much about the Bible, but I knew faith, repentance, confession and baptism and that's about all. But I would just march up one aisle and down the other, and dare anybody to say anything about what I was preaching. Just look a fellow in the eye, you know, and say, "Don't you believe what I'm telling you, what I am reading you from God's word? If you don't believe it just get up and tell these people about it." Once in a while a fellow would get up. Of course, that was good for me because that would always make me have to think a little more and do a little more preparation.

Now, friends, I don't mean that we have to be like that. I think we ought to always be ready to give every man an answer for the reason of the hope that is within us, with meekness and with fear all right, but I think it's a matter of being prepared, understanding that which God has said, not necessarily making a great show of it. I think we are going to have to fight in open warfare. For instance, with regard to the name of God's people: what is the name of the church, and what is the name of God's people? The Bible tells us the church is referred to as the *church*, the *church of God*, and *churches of Christ*. It was Jesus who said: "Upon this rock I will build my church; and the gates of hell shall not prevail against it." Now my point is this: The statement made by the Lord is a statement that demonstrates the fact that he was the builder, therefore, it is the church of Christ. It is the one that the Lord built. I'm not ashamed to defend that; I don't think you ought to be. I believe that God's teaching is, that is the organization the Lord built; that institution was built by him; that institution is the one that I am a member of, and I believe we have to tell people about it. Tell them in a nice way; just as nice as you can, but let them understand what is the teaching of the Bible with

regard to the church. Take the name of God's people.
I'm just a Christian. Listen to this: the Bible says the
disciples were called *Christians* first at Antioch, Acts
11:26.. And then in the 26th chapter of the same book
of Acts of Apostles, the 28th verse, Agrippa said, "Almost
thou persuadest me to be a *Christian.*" Peter said in I
Peter the 4th chapter and verse 16: "Yet if any man suffer as a *Christian,* let him not be ashamed; but let him
glorify God on this behalf." The American Standard Version says, "In this name." We ought to teach people that
they ought to be *Christians.* There is no authority for the
denominational names that people wear. Now of course
to the people who do not understand the teaching of the
Bible, this sometimes amazes them, that the denominational names that people wear are not accepted in the
sight of God.

Again, the plan of salvation has been a battle ground
upon which we have fought over and over again. The
Book teaches that people must believe in the Lord, and
believing in the Lord, they must turn away from sin and
be baptized for the remission of sins, having confessed
Christ before men. That is the teaching of the Bible concerning the plan of salvation.

Worship has always been a battle ground. Whether
or not we ought to use mechanical instruments of music
in the worship, for instance. What is God's authority?
Why, the Bible says sing. We have had to fight that kind
of fight all the way through. Now, friends, what is this?
I want you to see that the second battle ground is the
battle ground of open warfare.

I believe that we must be ready to give an answer to
every man that asks for that hope that we have. That
was the thing that these Jews were doing. When this
Sanballat and Tobiah stood out there on the plains and
said, Yah, yah, yah, these men just went ahead and built.
But when they said, Come on out and we'll fight you, they
laid down their tools and went to it. But of course there
was not any fighting? Why not ? Because the enemy was not

ready to meet Israel out there in open warfare, although Israel was ready. You know, there is a great thing, friends, in being ready, and I think we ought to do that with regard to the Bible, the Word of the living God.

I'm trying to get you to understand tonight that battle ground number two may be open warfare. And when the enemy says, "Let's get out here and have open warfare about this thing called the Word of the Living God," then we ought to even be ready for that, and we are. It may come just from an incident that may happen between you and your neighbor. Your neighbor may say, "Well, now then, I just don't believe that" (some point of religion).

You say, "Well, here is what the Book teaches."

Well you and that neighbor are crossing swords on something, and of course, the thing that you settle it by is not what you think, or what the preacher says, or what somebody has said in times past, but by what the Book teaches. And when you can do it that way, friends, then you are meeting the issue. These people were ready.

But listen again. I want to read another passage for you. Nehemiah 5:1-3 is the Old Testament reference— the New Testament reference is found in the book of Acts of Apostles and I Corinthians 6. Nehemiah says in the 5th chapter, verse 1, beginning: "And there was a great cry of the people and of their wives against their brethren the Jews." It looks like they are having trouble on the inside now. They have had trouble on the outside from ridicule and criticism, but now, something is happening inside the city.

They said: "We, our sons, and our daughters, are many: therefore we take up corn for them, that we may eat, and live. Some also there were that said, We have mortgaged our lands, vineyards, and houses, that we might buy corn, because of the dearth." And verse 6 says, "And I was very angry when I heard their cry and these words." Down in verse 12 it says, "We will restore them, and will require nothing of them, so we will do as thou sayest.

Then I called the priests, and took an oath of them, that they should do according to this promise."

Now here is the point: the third battle that they had to fight was internal trouble. Internal trouble! Well you know when you are building, sometimes that's true. The Book says, "I was very angry when I heard their cry." Nehemiah was very angry, but listen: he got results. He said to them, "You do this," and they said, "We will restore them and require nothing." Some had mortgaged their land to these scheming Jews that were inside the city, and they were going to take advantage of this situation. So Nehemiah just went up and said: "We will not have that. We are all brethren together here; we are not going to have this internal trouble, and this strife that is caused by your planning against your brethren." Thus the internal trouble was settled.

You know, friends, you are nearly always going to have something you are going to have to fight as you go through life. I want to turn over here to a passage in the New Testament, in I Corinthians 6:1 and read something to you that a lot of our brethren seem to have forgotten. Paul is writing to the church at Corinth and he says, among other things: "Dare any of you, having a matter against another, go to law before the unjust, and not before the saints?" What's the trouble? Why one of the brethren was evidently either suing or getting ready to sue another brother in the church. Paul pointed out to them: "That's not the way to handle things; that's not the way that these problems must be settled." Thus they had to fight internal disturbances.

Did you ever notice a bride and groom as they have just been married, as they go off on their honeymoon in a shower of rice, how happy they are as they go away? They go off on a honeymoon and stay a few days or a week, or maybe a couple of weeks, and they come back and settle down to housekeeping, after he has carried her across the threshold into the new apartment, or the new home, or wherever they are going to live. She looks at him and he looks at her and they say to each other: "Honey, we are never going to have any trouble. Everything is going to be all right." But you know, time goes by and pretty soon they get down to the bed rock of living. By and by little disturbances arise that must be settled, and they are settled if they have built on a solid foundation, if they have built on a proper foundation. There is always the danger of internal disturbances in the home—always things to be settled. I have heard husbands and wives say that they have never had any disagreements, "We never have any disagreements." I often wonder if they ever accomplish anything. You know, I believe most of us are so constructed that we do have some disturbances sometimes. Of course, I always settle everything in my family (or think I do) and we don't have any trouble with any of those matters. I claim my scriptural prerogative as the head of the family, but my wife sometimes comes back with the statement that she is the neck, so under that sort of an arrangement we get along wonderfully well!

Now my point is this: I believe that the church, the family of God, has to be careful about internal disturbances. You remember the statement that Paul made in the 20th chapter of the book of the Acts of Apostles? He said, "And from among your own selves shall men arise, speaking perverse things, to draw away the disciples after them." Now what are you going to do when that happens? Have you ever had any kind of trouble like that here in the Clearwater church? Have you ever had a man arise to speak some kind of a perverse thing to draw away disciples after him? Is that something foreign to the churches in Florida? God knows it isn't. There have been dozens, I believe I could say, of individuals who have caused internal trouble in the church, and we have had to fight on that battle ground in the past just as we will have to fight on that same battle ground in the future. And we need to be prepared.

My friends, I trust that you can appreciate these principles that I am trying to get before you tonight. I want you to see that although internal strife came among the people of Israel, and it will come among God's people to-day. Even those things that cause strife between brethren, they can be settled in the church just as husband and wife settle their difficulties in the home. The elders should settle such problems and difficulties among the family of God because they want to win the victory on this battle ground of internal disturbance and trouble. But we need to be prepared.

But there is one more battle ground that I want to mention. I'm now looking at Nehemiah 6, verse 1: "Now it came to pass, when Sanballat, and Tobiah, and Geshem the Arabian, and the rest of our enemies, heard that I had builded the wall, and that there was no breach left therein; (though at that time I had not set up the doors upon the gates;) that Sanballat and Geshem sent unto me, saying, Come, let us meet together in some one of the villages in the plain of Ono. But they thought to do me mischief. And I sent messengers unto them, saying, I am doing a great work, so that I cannot come down: why should the work cease, whilst I leave it, and come down to you? Yet they sent unto me four times after this sort: and I answered them after the same manner."

Now what is that battle ground? It is the battle ground of compromise. "Come down now in one of the villages of the plain of Ono and let us talk this thing over." That is without doubt the most dangerous of them all. You know, I'm not so worried about losing the battle of ridicule as we find it on the first battle ground. I'm not uneasy about whether or not we will win the battle in open warfare. I know that we will. When men go out with the sword of the Spirit, God's word is never defeated in open warfare or any other kind of warfare. I am not uneasy, therefore, about the idea of ridicule getting the better of too many of us. It will destroy some. I'm not uneasy about winning the battle on the plains out yonder as we engage in open warfare with the enemy. Of course, I'm worried about internal strife, but not as much as I am this fourth battle ground, the battle ground of compromise. Listen friends, if we are losing the battle at all in the church that the Lord died to establish, it is on the ground of compromise. Why? I don't believe that many of you people here are going to compromise the truth, the Word of God. I don't think that you will do that. I'm afraid that you may compromise your time. The devil monopolizes our time more and more as the days go by. We are compromising with the devil with regard to our time. Now you think about yourself. What about the amount of time that you spend now in the service of the Lord and the amount of time that you spent in His service, for example, the first year or two that you were a member of the body of Christ? How about your time? How much of it do you devote NOW as compared to the amount of time that you formerly devoted? I am not uneasy about my brethren changing the plan of salvation. I am concerned, of course, about the fact that modernism is creeping into the church, and we could have a lot to say about that. But I am not really as uneasy about that as I am compromise. Compromising not only time, but compromising with the world. We have friends, people who are out there in the world, that have a tremendous influence over us. They say to us, "Well, it seems to me that you could do this or you could do that." By and by we succumb to the appeals of compromise, and when we do, there isn't but one result and that result is that we are going to sacrifice our faith.

I know a splendid young lady who has been on my mind almost constantly for the last 24 hours. She is a very fine girl, a faithful member of the church. I learned last evening a little earlier than this that she had married an individual who apparently is not concerned about the church. She wasn't even able to get him to come to the services yesterday on her wedding day. She may be loyal, she may even win her husband, and I pray God that she will, but I think she has taken the first step along the route of compromise. Not simply because of the fact that she has married out of the church, but because of the fact that she has already allowed that, and allowed him to interfere with her activity as a child of God. He is a member of the Roman Catholic Church. We had arranged to have a meeting between a priest and some gospel preachers in the presence of both of them with the hope that this young man who doesn't know much about his doctrine might see the truth of the Lord. But I am persuaded that she has compromised, which is going to make her life much more difficult than if she had stood firm and tried to show him the truth of God until a sufficient amount of time had elapsed that she could have tried to make an impression upon him. Friends, it doesn't make any difference about the specific example; what matters is whether or not that we understand what is the meaning of compromise. When any set of forces asks me to come down in the plains of Ono and to discuss this matter, that is, to compromise this matter, it is a sad situation. Then people lose a battle on the battle ground of compromise.

I'm going to read another passage for you and then the sermon is over. In Nemiah the 6th chapter and verse 16 it says: "And it came to pass, that when all our enemies heard thereof, and all the heathen that were about us saw these things," (that's the building up of the walls) "they were much cast down in their own eyes." Now watch! "For they perceived that this work was wrought of our God." They perceived that the work was wrought of our God. Now my last one is this: If you win the battle on the battle ground of ridicule and criticism; if you win the battle on the battle ground of open warfare; if you win the battle on the battle ground of internal strife and trouble inside the body of Christ; if you win the battle on the battle ground of compromise, God is the basis for your victory. It was Paul who said, I can do all things through Christ who strengthens me. Thus, because of His strength, because of His power, we can win these battles as we fight them day by day with the various enemies that present themselves to us.

Now then, my friends, tonight I wonder if you are having any kind of a fight at all. Members of the church say to me, "Brother Pickup, the devil never bothers me." Do you know what I say to those people? I say, "Brother, Sister, maybe you are not bothering the devil. Maybe you are not giving him any trouble, so he is leaving you alone."

You know, the devil is a wonderful felow to leave well enough alone. If an individual is going along and not making any fuss about anything; if he isn't opposing Satan at all but is willing to fall in with anything that Satan suggests, and if Satan can almost whip him on any field of battle with which he may cross swords, then he will let him continue as he is. But if you are really doing something; if you are really getting out there and making some progress in the work of the Lord, then, friends, Satan is going to give you some trouble. Do you have any people in the world who try to prevent you from doing the Lord's will? Do you have any friends who try to suggest to you that this is not too important? Do individuals argue with you about the Scriptures and say, "Now I just don't believe this is true and that is true," when God's Divine Word teaches it so plainly? Do you allow a thing like that to go by? My friends, you are losing the battle and don't know it. I want you to think about that tonight.

The cause of Christ today in Florida and every where else depends upon whether or not we are winning the battles on these battle grounds that have been suggested on this ocacsion. It depends upon whether or not that we are winning THESE battles. And thus, as we lose them, we are losing more and more ground.

I go into some places and see the cause barely alive and say to myself: "Which one of the battles are these people losing here at this place?" I go into another place and we see a great deal of worldliness and I say, "Which one of the battles are the people of this congregation losing?" Now here is my point: You ask yourself the question tonight, my friends: "Which one of the battles am I losing?" If I am losing any, which one? I think about conditions as we see them about us and I say to myself, "Where have I missed the point with regard to this particular matter?" I wonder where I missed it with regard to that young lady I mentioned a moment ago? Where did I miss it with regard to my instruction to her? I must have missed it somewhere. The elders must have missed it somewhere; the whole church must have missed it somewhere, but where did we miss it? We lost the battle, at least we have thus far. And so, it is sometimes individual.

Not only does the church lose a battle, but individuals lose battles. Sometimes a father and a mother lose a battle with regard to a child, and that child marches off, leaves the church, forgets the Cause of Christ, forsakes its first love, turns away from the principles of right. Now where did that father and mother lose the fight? These are challenging thoughts. They are not something that you can throw over your shoulder and say, "Well, we are not engaged in a fight; there are no battle grounds." I affirm to you that we HAVE these battle grounds that I have suggested.

But the lesson is before you. I want you to apply these things to your own hearts and say to yourself, "Am I winning or am I losing? If I am losing, then God help me to strengthen myself and fight harder than I have ever fought before, to the end that God may be glorified, His Cause built up, and men and women edified in the church of the Lord Jesus Christ."

If you are here tonight and you are not a Christian, you haven't won a single battle. You haven't won a single battle. If you are out of Christ, if you are not a member of the organization about which the Lord said, "Upon this rock I will build my church," then you need to win battle number one by hearing, believing and obeying the gospel of the Lord Jesus Christ in spite of anything that anybody might say to the contrary. I think that I can remember when I obeyed the gospel. Not a single member of my family was concerned about my obedience to the gospel of Christ. But I was concerned about my soul, and because I was concerned about it, I went ahead anyhow in spite of the fact that neither my father nor my mother were interested. I won battle number one at that time in spite of the silent ridicule of my parents. And then, later there came another battle and that was the battle of open warfare. I didn't know much about the church, about God, about the teaching of Christ, but I did my best in my feeble way to win that battle. How successful I was only God knows, but I tried throughout the years to win the various encounters with the opposition.

Sometimes there comes into an individual's life internal strife: a fighting with one's self. Paul said, "I buffet my body and bring it into subjection." That's an internal fight, individually. We must fight that one too. Paul said he did. Sometimes we have to fight with compromise. You, individually, have got to do that. I suggest to you, friends, that you turn these things over in your minds and apply them to yourselves however they may fit your particular case. If you are not a Christian, win the first battle tonight by obeying the gospel. If you are out of duty, win which ever battle that you are fighting, and come back to the church. Confess your faults one to another; pray one for another that you may be healed. If you are a subject of the invitation won't you come while together we stand and sing?

THE SPIRIT OF CHRIST

We come again tonight, friends, to talk for a little while about some things that are eternal, and to suggest to those of you who are here some matters for your consideration concerning a most important subject. I have selected as the lesson for tonight, as has already been announced, the statement that was made by Paul to the church at Rome, beginning with verse 5 of the 8th chapter of Romans. He says, "For they that are after the flesh do mind the things of the flesh; but they that are after the Spirit the things of the Spirit. For to be carnally minded is death; but to be spiritually minded is life and peace. Because the carnal mind is enmity against God: for it is not subject to the law of God, neither indeed can be. So then they that are in the flesh cannot please God. But ye are not in the flesh, but in the Spirit, if so be that the Spirit of God dwell in you. Now if any man have not the Spirit of Christ, he is none of His."

I believe this is a most important subject, and that the apostle to the Gentiles deals with it in these passages in a very clear cut and concise manner. I think that the expressions that are used here need no special exegesis for it is clear, almost from the beginning of the paragraph, that he is speaking about the spirit of Christ that men ought to walk after, and to walk not after the ways of the flesh. Paul recognized the fact that man lives in the flesh. He is not trying to present some strange doctrine that, while we are living, we are not living in the flesh. He doesn't mean that. He simply means that as we live in the flesh we are not to try to please the flesh, but to walk according to the spirit of Christ and not according to the spirit of the flesh. Now if I can understand what is the spirit of Christ, then I am able to live the kind of a life that God wants me to live. In fact, it is impossible for me to live as God wants me to live except as I have the spirit, as Paul says, of Christ. I believe that you and I can profitably spend some time tonight in a discussion of this thought, or this theme. That is the reason that I have selected it early in the meeting.

I think that, although maybe most of you are members of the church, you and I need to think about this possession, that is a cherished possession, the possession of Christ's spirit. What does it mean? Most people have rather peculiar ideas about what is the spirit of Christ. In fact many times people say, "I don't think you are manifesting the spirit of Christ." Now I recognize the fact that sometimes people do not always manifest the spirit of Christ. I'm aware of that. I dare say that sometimes we will become angry or perturbed over a matter and we let the devil become the ruling influence in our lives. We ought not to do that. But the Bible teaches that when we so sin we have an advocate with the Father, and the thing for us to do is to repent of that, pray God for forgiveness, and then try to manifest the spirit of the Master. The trouble is that some ideas about this are so far removed from the teaching of the gospel that we need to correct the ideas that people have, even among us, regarding the spirit of Christ. I read in the Bible that if one does not have the spirit of Christ he is none of His. I think that Paul simply means that he is not a Christian. I don't believe a man is a Christian who isn't in possession of the spirit of Christ. Neither do I think that that individual is saved from sin. You can't have the spirit of the devil and accidentally obey God. You can't do that. You have to obey Christ, obey God, with the spirit of Christ. I likewise think that the person who does not possess Christ's spirit will not enter heaven at last. Thus you can see it is important; and you and I need to think about this, and the world needs to think about it, so we ought to preach it. If tonight I can indoctrinate further those of us who are members of the church, so that we who are Christians have more of the spirit of the Master, then I ought to do that. First of all, if one is not a Christian he does not possess the spirit of Christ. Second, if he is not saved from sin, he is not a Christian; and third, certainly he can never go to heaven. Thus we see, friends, it is important that individuals possess the spirit as is outlined in the Bible.

I would like to say further, by way of getting this matter clearly before us, that when an individual obeys the gospel, he must have the spirit of the Master. You can not obey God and have any other spirit. You can't have any other purpose in mind, and we are going to talk about that on the subject of obedience tonight, because we must have the spirit of the Lord as we obey God. Neither can we possess that spirit and violate God's will. We are going to walk by His will if we have His spirit. When we walk according to the will of God, we are walking in the way that God says we ought to walk.

I have put down a little memorandum that I picked up somewhere that is said to be the writing of Albert Barnes. Here is what he says about the spirit of Christ: "If a man is not influenced by the pure and holy spirit of the Lord Jesus, if he is not conformed to His image, if his life does not resemble that of the Saviour, he is a stranger to religion. He may be loud in his profession, amiable in his temper, bold in his zeal or active in promoting the interests of his own party. But if he has not the temper of the Saviour and does not manifest His spirit, it is as a sounding brass or a tinkling symbal." Now I think, at least to some extent, that rather expresses the idea in sort of a summation of the things that I want to say tonight regarding the spirit of the Lord Jesus Christ.

First of all I want to be as concrete as I can; I want you to be able to get your teeth into what I am saying; and I want to make it so certain that I am going to emphasize these statements by beginning each thought with a positive affirmation of the principle that I want you to see. First, then, I want to call your attention to a passage of Scripture in I Peter 2:21-23 which says: "For even hereunto were ye called: because Christ also suffered for us, leaving us an example, that ye should follow His steps: who did no sin, neither was guile found in his mouth: who, when he was reviled, reviled not again; when he suffered, he threatened not; but committed himself to him that judgeth righteously." Then there is another one. In the Book of Luke, 23rd chapter and verse 34, the Son of God is dying on the cross and He says: "Father, forgive them; for they know not what they do." Now my first thought, therefore, tonight, is the spirit of the Lord Jesus Christ concerning personal injury and insult. If you can break down the idea into its different parts, if you can see how the Lord manifested himself toward personal injury and insult, then you are able to know what was the temper of Jesus, what was his demeanor, what spirit he manifested when he was injured personally by the individuals who mocked him, and who were actually responsible for his death upon the cross.

Look at the statement I read from I Peter 2 again. It says, "Leaving us an example, that ye should follow his steps." Peter said that guile was not found in his mouth; that he did not revile those who reviled him; that although he suffered, he threatened not. but he committed himself to him that judgeth righteously. Now there, my friends, is the spirit of the Lord. Can you exercise yourselves concerning personal insult and injury with regard to that? That is the One who on the cross was able to say: "Father, forgive them; for they know not what they do;" who had previously said to the people as he taught them in the sermon on the mount, "If a man smite thee on the one cheek, turn to him the other also." That is the Christ who is living for our example, and I suggest to you, my friends, that you and I can profit by a little more of the appropriation of that spirit that he possessed, and that possessed Him while He lived upon this earth.

But I want you to notice still another statement that is made in the New Testament regarding a second idea about the spirit of Christ. In Mark the 10th chapter and verse 45 the record says: "For even the Son of man came not to be ministered unto, but to minister." Then I read in the 13th chapter of the gospel of John that, "If I then, your Lord and Master, have washed your feet; ye also ought to wash one another's feet." Now what is he talking about? Why, he is referring to the menial task that he had just performed when he went about with a towel and a basin of water washing the tired and dusty feet of the disciples as an act of service unto them.

Sometimes people get confused on the subject of feet washing, so I want to spend just a moment or two discussing it. I think we have smiled at the idea or ridiculed the thought to the extent that we have lost sight of the meaning of the passage. There is no reason for us to back off from any passage that the Lord has given us as an example. I spent a great deal of time over in the Eastern section of North Carolina several years ago in what we would refer to as a **Free Will Baptist Community.** The Free Will Baptists were very strong in that neighborhood. They had their regular meetings in which they met together to wash feet as an act of worship unto God. I had a radio program every day, so I dealt with those things trying to show what was the teaching of the Lord with regard to that Scripture. Now we have laughed it off time and time again, but I believe in feet washing. And I am not using that in a humorous sense. I believe in it. I think that the Church of God today does practice it, not as an act of worship unto God, because it never was an act of worship. I think the spirit of humility and the spirit of service that characterized the Lord on that occasion should characterize us today. What does he mean when he says: "If I then, your Lord and Master, have washed your feet; ye also ought to wash one another's feet"? Why listen: don't you remember the statement that was made by Paul to Timothy in writing about the widows? He said: "If she have brought up children, if she have lodged strangers, if she have washed the saints' feet." What does that mean? Why that simply means, has this widow been faithful in service to others? Not has she taken off her shoes and stockings in the meeting house and then exposed clean, white feet that have been scrubbed, scrupulously clean before coming to service, and then have someone go through the motions of washing feet that have already been washed. That is mockery in the sight of God. That is not feet washing; that is going through the **motions** of doing something. The feet of these disciples on this occasion—in John 13—needed washing. These humble servants of God received a blessing from the Master who was willing to humiliate himself to the point of washing the feet of his disciples.

Now I don't like to take up time with this in a sermon such as this tonight, but I wanted you to see that inasmuch as I have introduced the Scripture, what is the meaning of it? It is simply an act of service unto your fellowman, not an act of worship to God. You couldn't worship God by washing my feet. If you washed everybody's feet in the community you would still be right where you were so far as worship to God is concerned. You can serve your fellowman in all kinds of acts of service; yes, even to the extent of being humble enough to bathe the body of that individual whose body needs your care, who may perchance be unable to provide it for himself. But let's not be engaged in mockery. What was the spirit of the Lord concerning service to other? He said: "If I, your Lord and Master, have served, then you ought to serve. If I have gone out and helped people, you ought to go out and help them." God knows that today, brethren and friends, we can relearn that lesson. We can see what His spirit was concerning service to other people, and we can emulate His example, we can profit from His teaching, and certainly we ought to do that.

Let me read another one. In Philippians the 2nd chapter, verses 5 through 7, he said: "Have this mind in you, which was also in Christ Jesus: who, existing in the form of God, counted not the being on an equality with God a thing to be grasped, but emptied himself, taking the form of a servant, being made in the likeness of men." Now what do we have there? Look at the expression! There is one of the strongest terms in the Bible. The Lord EMPTIED himself of his divinity and came down to this low land of sin and sorrow and became a man. That was a step down for the Lord. You know, sometimes I think of the statement that was made by Paul on this occasion, when the Lord emptied himself, and I think about the Lord as he left the courts of glory and what heaven had to give up in order that Christ might come down and spend a third of a century among the people of this earth. Thus, the Lord emptied himself of his divinity; he left heaven and its glory and came down to this earth to become a servant.

But that is not all. I want you to notice a statement in Romans the 12th chapter and verse 10. He says: "Be kindly affectioned one to another with brotherly love; in honour preferring one another." Friends, that is the spirit of the Lord concerning service to others. It simply means that he was anxious to show people that he considered himself a servant, and that he considered other people the recipients of blessings that he could offer; and likewise he points out to us that these individuals **needed** the blessings that He could give. We also should be willing and anxious to give them. We are to be kindly affectioned one toward another in honor preferring one another. Now that's the spirit of the Lord; that's the spirit of Christ concerning service to other people.

This past year when school was opened at Florida Christian College, Brother Cope made a statement that he picked up somewhere along the way that I thought was a classic, and I haven't forgotten it. He told the story of a young man who was a real success in his school life, and when he had finished some course that he had been taking, some of his room mates in the same building came to inquire concerning the secret of his success. For a long, long time he was unwilling to make the statement that he did make to them finally; and it was almost by accident that the statement was obtained. Somebody discovered the young man's motto, and it was this: "I want to be third. God first, others second, myself third." You know, that is a classic; that is the teaching of the Bible regarding service to others. The Lord Jesus Christ possessed that spirit; you and I must likewise possess it if we are to have the spirit of the Lord.

The third major principle that I wish to call to our attention this evening is the spirit of the Lord Jesus Christ regarding obedience. Now this is a big item with me. It is also important with the Bible because the Bible makes it clear that obedience is a most important subject. Listen to this. In Philippians 2:8 Paul says: "And being found in a fashion as a man, he" (referring to the Lord) "humbled himself, and became obedient unto death, even the death of the cross." In Hebrews 5:8,9: "Though he were a Son, yet learned he obedience by the things which he suffered; and being made perfect, he became the author of eternal salvation unto all them that obey him." And then another passage is found over here in John the 3rd chapter in which we find the Lord discussing the idea of the New Birth, and He instructs Nicodemus that he too must become obedient. Jesus said: "Except a man be born again he cannot see the kingdom of God."

Nicodemus said: "Can I enter my mother's womb when I am old and be born again?"

The Lord replied in John 3:5: "Verily, verily, I say unto thee, Except a man be born of water and of the Spirit, he cannot enter into the kingdom of God."

Now watch, my friends, over here in the passage I read in Philippians 2, the Bible says that Christ was willing to become obedient unto death, even the death of the cross. Then in the Hebrew letter, chapter 5, verses 8,9: "Although he were a Son, yet learned he obedience by the things which he suffered; and being made perfect, he became the author of eternal salvation unto all them that obey him." Now watch. Nicodemus was instructed to the end that if he expected to go to heaven, he had to be born again. Likewise, when the Lord was about to leave this earth, he said to his disciples: "Go ye into all the world, and preach the gospel to every creature. He that believeth and is baptized shall be saved; but he that believeth not shall be damned." The point is this: You can't possibly have the spirit of the Lord unless you have his spirit with regard to obedience. Jesus was willing to suffer, even death,

the death of the cross. And although willing to suffer
the death of the cross, the Bible says that by suffering,
or through suffering, he became the author of salvation.
To whom? To those who are willing to obey him. You
can't have the spirit that some do with regard to obedience
and go to heaven when life is over. Why not? Because
Paul said that except you have the spirit of Christ you are
none of his. For some individual to point out, "Well, I
just can't see any sense in this, and I can't understand the
other," is equal to saying, "Well, I'm just not willing to
obey him." Now watch one other statement. The same
thing is said by Peter in Acts 2:38: "Repent, and be baptized every one of you in the name of Jesus Christ for the
remission of sins, and ye shall receive the gift of the Holy
Ghost." Somebody says, "Oh, yes, I know that's in the
Bible, but I think we ought to emphasize the essentials
such as love, and faith, and joy and peace." No, friends,
you don't think that people ought to emphasize such things
as that. You just don't have the spirit of Christ. Look
at it for just a minute. The Bible says that the Lord Jesus
Christ had the spirit of obedience. Now you must have
the spirit of obedience. Although he obeyed by dying on
the cross, he doesn't expect that of you. He only expects
that you become obedient unto Him and live the Christian
life. But now you notice this. The Bible says—and Jesus
is the author of the expression—that faith in Christ is an
essential. Well, we can understand that. He also says that
repentance is an essential. He likewise teaches that baptism is also essential. Some people say, "Oh, well, I can
understand and see through the idea of faith all right. And
I can see through the idea of repentance all right. But I
can't see through the idea of baptism." Let me tell you,
brother, if that's your attitude, it is not a question of what
you do or do not see, it is a question of the spirit of Christ
which you lack! There is your trouble, and you are going
to be lost because you don't have the spirit of Christ. You
are not going to hell because you were not baptized; you
are not going to be lost in hell because you didn't take the

Lord's Supper; you are going to be lost because you didn't have the spirit of Christ concerning obedience!

Paul said, "If any man have not the spirit of Christ, he is none of his." That individual who backs off and says that love is one of the essentials, that faith is one of the essentials, that peace is one of the essentials, doesn't have to worry about what is essential; he just doesn't have the spirit of Christ. Suppose you were to be the recipient of an estate that was left you by your father according to certain terms of his will. One of the terms of his will was that you believe: that you have faith in him as your earthly father, and that you recognize him as such by your conduct relative to the rest of the family and to his memory. You would say, "All right, I can do that." Suppose that the terms of the will demanded that in order for you to receive this estate you are going to have to turn away from the ungodly practices that you have been engaged in. You have been living a wild, wicked life; you have been a wayward son. But the old man is still and cold in death and already buried by the time they are probating his will. The lawyer gets up and says: "Listen here, buddy, if you want to get any of this money, you have to mend your ways." There would be a lot of fast mending done if the estate involved much money. That is because you have to satisfy the terms of the will. The same thing would be true concerning any other process, even if it required of you that you go through some kind of a form that he would describe as baptism, and the result of it would be that you would receive the estate. Thus the whole thing would depend upon whether or not you had rendered obedience unto the terms of your father's will to receive the money, you would not take any chances about it, but you would go through the thing exactly as your father had stated in his will, and you would be a fool if you didn't.

But you know, lots of people think, "Well, I think we ought to have the spirit of the Lord all right. We ought to have His spirit, but I don't think it is necessary to emphasize these things." Listen, brother, Christ emphasized obedience and stamped it with His own spirit. "Although he were a Son," God demanded of him that he obey. Because he obeyed he became the author of the salvation that is mine if I obey him. Now what are the terms of it? Well, the Bible says that except you believe in the Lord, you are going to be damned. Hebrew 11:6: "Without faith it is impossible to please him: for he that cometh to God must believe that he is, and that he is a rewarder of them that diligently seek him." Then again we have the expression in 17th chapter of Acts and verse 30: "And the times of this ignorance God winked at; but now commandeth all men every where to repent." Now that is demanded of you. Then the Bible says: "He that believeth and is baptized shall be saved." The person who doesn't believe that is damned because of the lack of faith in Christ. So faith is essential. In the 22nd chapter of the book of Acts and verse 16: "And now why tarriest thou? Arise, and be baptized, and wash away thy sins, calling on the name of the Lord." Then in I Peter the 3rd chapter and verse 21: "The like figure whereunto even baptism doth also now save us." Friends, I don't see how a person can say he has obeyed God and then repudiate those things.

I heard a fellow say one time, "I would not mind being a Christian"—just think about putting it like that—"I would not mind being a Christian." You know, some people think they are doing God a favor when they obey the gospel. "I would not mind obeying the gospel," this fellow said, "if I didn't have to be baptized." You know what I said to him, as I recall it? Why, I said to him, "You could be put 25 feet under water and you would just go down a dry sinner and come up a wet one so far as your obedience to God is concerned." What is wrong with that kind of a man? He has got to have the spirit of obedience. The Lord said we are to do this and he left these examples that we need to follow in order that we may be saved.

I want you to notice still another principle. I want you to see the spirit of Christ regarding his Father's word. In Matthew 21 and verses 12 and 13, Jesus went and cast out

all of them that sold—into the temple mind you—and over-
threw the tables of the money changers. In the 23rd chapter of the same book and verse 33, he denounced the Pharisees with the statement: "Ye serpents, ye generation of
vipers, how can ye escape the damnation of hell?" What is
that? That is the spirit of Christ. You say, "Well, that
doesn't look like the spirit of Christ to me." Well, I'll tell
you friends, that is the spirit of the Lord according to the
teaching of the Bible! It is not necessarily the spirit that
sometimes men want to discuss as the spirit of Christ. We
like to think of the Lord as the meek and lowly man from
Nazareth. I want to say smething else that I have said
a few times recently, and I shall doubtless say many more
times before I die. One thing that almost gives me a chill
is to look at some of the pictures that I see of the Lord
with that weak, sickly expression on his face: that shallow
complexion and the feminine expression, and hear people
tell little children that it is the picture of the Lord. That's
not a picture of my Lord! That's not a picture of Jesus of
Nazareth, the Son of God. Why, friends, he was a man's
man. He was not a feminine type of individual. He wasn't
a person who didn't know which side that he was on and
looked about to see what was the pulse of public opinion
before he took a position. He was the Lion of Judah in
that particular case, by the way. Yes, he was the meek
and lowly man from Nazareth too. He was a man who could
go into a home and put his hand on the head of little children and bless them; and little boys and girls came about
him because they loved him. He radiated friendliness. He
was able to go and talk to people who were bereaved and
comfort them as he did Mary and Martha at the tomb of
Lazarus, and he himself wept on that occasion. He was
one who could be touched by the feelings of our infirmities,
but he was also one who could stand up as the Lion of
Judah and denounce those filthy Pharisees to their teeth
and say, "You generation of vipers." You know, I never
have used language like that. I have had it said to me that
sometimes in my denunciation of error that I didn't have the

spirit of Christ. I have never in my life said the things the
Lord said on that occasion; I couldn't say them because I
don't know the minds of people like he did. But he said,
"You are whited sepulchres." Do you know what he meant
by that? He is talking about rotting human flesh inside
of a tomb where the body is buried. If you should go inside where that filthy, rotting body is you couldn't stand
the odor. On the outside of the tomb it is beautiful and
white, but inside the maggots are eating the bodies of the
people who have died. Jesus said, "That's the kind of folk
you are." That, my friends, is the spirit of Christ. That
is the spirit of Christ denouncing error when people were
violating his Father's Word.

Oh, yes, when they slapped him on the one cheek, he
was able to turn the other. When they demanded of him
his coat, he was able to give his cloak also. When they required him to go a mile, he could go two. He said the disciples were supposed to do that, and they were, and we are.
But when his Father's Word was called in question, and
when his Father's Word was being violated by wicked men
who were leading people away from the truth of the gospel,
then he stood up before them and called them what they
were. That, my brother, is the spirit of Christ against
those who were refuting or attempting to refute his
Father's Word. My friends, do you see what it means to
have the spirit of Christ?

Now let me get one other point here and then we will
pass. In the 7th chapter of the Book of Acts of Apostles
and verse 51, I want you to see the spirit of Christ as it
dwelt in the martyr Stephen. Stephen began to speak to
the people. He told them about the things that their
fathers had done, and then he finally came to the climax
because these wicked Jews were standing there ready to
denounce the very words he was preaching. He said, "Ye
stiffnecked and uncircumcised in heart and ears, ye do always resist the Holy Spirit: as your fathers did, so do ye."
They put him to death because he said it. Was Stephen
right or wrong? Was Stephen following the spirit of the

Lord? Yes! We saw Christ as he was denouncing the Pharisees and now we see Stephen denouncing the same group of wicked Jews. Christ and Stephen have the identical spirit, and I'm going to show you what I mean by that. The Lord denounced their wickedness in withstanding the word of God; he drove them out of the temple; he said, "You have made my Father's house a house of merchandise, you are wicked, you are unprincipled men." Stephen stood up in the presence of the same individuals, at least some of the same kind of folk, and said: "Ye stiffnecked and uncircumcised in heart and ears, ye do always resist the Holy Ghost: as your fathers did, so do ye." They crucified the Lord Jesus Christ and he raised his voice to his Father and he said, "Father, while I have withstood them as they attacked your Word, and while I tried to preach to them the ways of right and show them wherein they had make a mistake, they put me to death. Father, I want you to forgive these people." That was the Lord. Now listen to Stephen. He had pronounced the woes upon them because of their wickedness, and they stoned him to death. The Bible says that he actually looked up and saw the Son of God standing on the right hand of the Father, and he said almost the same words the Lord said: "Lord, lay not this sin to their charge." Think about that. The spirit on one hand of obedience unto God with respect to the Word of God, and the spirit on the other hand with regard to personal insult and personal injury. With regard to personal injury, he is the Lamb of God; with regard to his Father's Word, he is the Lion of Judah. Do you see the spirit of Christ? That made a tremendous impression upon Saul of Tarsus. He was standing there beholding this scene and holding the garments of the people who laid down their coats as they stoned Stephen. Later in Acts 22nd chapter and verse 20 Paul says: "And when the blood of thy martyr Stephen was shed, I also was standing by, and consenting unto his death, and kept the raiment of them that slew him." That made an impression upon him. Listen: I'm going to venture an opinion tonight with regard to this. I think the spirit of Stephen so impressed Saul of Tarsus that it not only affected him then, but it may have had some effect upon him in becoming a follower of Christ, I believe that could have been true.

Now then in conclusion I want to read a passage that Paul writes tenderly when he says: "Let this mind be in you, which was also in Christ Jesus." Do you know what he means by that? He means that the man that is conformed to the image of Christ has the mind of Christ and the spirit of Christ. Do you know what you and I need to do more of with regard to these matters? We are going to have to appropriate from God's divine word more of the spirit of the Lord with regard to number one: our attitude toward insult and injury—personal reflection toward us. Oh how difficult that is for most of us. When someone requires that I turn the other cheek, I want to come up fighting. I don't like to turn the other cheek. That is repulsive to me. When someone strikes me on one cheek, there flares up in my bosom a spirit of vengeance that wants to settle this matter with my own hands and thus get vengeance upon this individual myself, but the spirit of the Lord says, "Down, down." That is a personal injury, so I must have more of the spirit of Christ.

Sometimes a man comes along and he makes fun of my Father's Word and I'm prone to excuse that because I do not want to get in an argument. I need more of the spirit of the Lord. Jesus would not have allowed that to happen. Yet sometimes I will stand by while somebody says something about my Father's Word that is absolutely false. I'm not nearly so ill tempered about that as I am about personal injury. You know, we just feel like we must reverse the thing. We must have more of the spirit of Christ regarding our Father's Word.

You know, friends, modernism is creeping into the church. Men are coming to say: "Oh, yes, I know that is what the Bible says about it, but the Bible is an inaccurate account of things; you can't always depend upon the written word of God." We just say, "Well, yes, I know, it's a matter of understanding: it's a matter of opinion." Opinion nothing! It is a matter of what God teaches with regard to this matter. I have no right to an opinion concerning something that is a direct violation of God's divine will. I am a patient individual in many things, but I have changed my ways concerning some of these matters whereof I speak tonight. I know I have been in homes where I would sit down and talk with people and watch their sneering smiles of contempt for God's divine will I would stay there and plug away trying to get them to see things differently. But you know how I do it now? Of course, I'm older now than I was when I used to do the other way. I go into a home and I talk patiently with people about the gospel. I try to have the spirit of my Master in presenting the will of God unto them just as kindly as I can. I do that with those who are in error concerning God's will; but when I come to an individual who sneers at God's Word, who will say to me: "Yes, I know that's what the Bible says, but I don't believe it." I shake hands with him, and I say: "Goodbye, brother, I'm on my way." Any individual who will look a plain, positive Scripture in the face and say: "Yes, that's what the Bible says, but I don't believe it," I say goodbye to him. I have finished my course so far as that individual is concerned. Let me tell you this: I don't have anything but the Word of God in my plea to individuals. I don't know how to fix it so that people will swallow it. I only know what God has said about it.

A few years ago a young gospel preacher was preaching his first sermon, and he preached that memorable sermon that Peter preached on Pentecost concerning which nobody would be able to improve, certainly not that young man. And he preached it as fervently as he knew how. There was a large crowd of people present that embarrassed him to some extent, and although he waxed warm toward the close of his sermon—preachers have a way of doing that you know—finally he finished. The people were standing around talking and he was just ready to go down off the stand and out of the building, when a large woman who had been sitting in the back of the small house elbowed her way down through the crowd and right up to the preacher. "Young man," she said, "you said that baptism is for the remission of sins."

By that time the young preacher was scared and he said, "I don't think that I said it."

She said, "Yes you did. You said that baptism is for the remission of sins, and I don't believe that."

"Well," he said, "Madam, I don't think that I said it, but," he said, "I did read what Peter said on the day of Pentecost."

She stopped for just an instant and then said, "Aw, shaw, I never did like old Peter's religion no how," and went out.

That is one way of getting rid of it. If you don't like what Paul said on the subject of the Lord's Supper, tear it out and throw it away. When you come over to what James said on the subject of works—"Faith without works is dead, being alone,"—just tear it out! The Bible says: "Ye shall then know that by works a man is justified, and not by faith only," so we tear out that statement because we don't like old James' way. I met a man the day before yesterday and he said, "I know an individual who has repudiated the entire book of James on the grounds that it doesn't quite conform to Paul's good old way of teaching on the subject of salvation by faith only, and so I don't accept James' teaching on the matter." Now how do you handle folk like that? Well, I'll tell you—there is not but one way to do it—just let those individuals that are going to tear the Bible up anyway, go on to the devil!

Now I try to teach people the truth, and I am going to instruct them in the way of the Lord to the best of my ability. When individuals are so misusing my Father's Word, I know but one course and that is to denounce their false teachings and show them that those things are wrong. I believe that is the spirit of Christ, without which I can't be saved. I want to conform to his image. I want to have the mind in me that was in Christ concerning personal injury and insult; concerning service to others; concerning my Father's Word; with regard to obedience unto God. Now if I can keep those things in mind and have the spirit of the Lord regarding them, then I can become and be one of his and go to heaven when life here is over.

Are you here tonight thinking you have the spirit and yet not willing to obey his will? Do you think some things are essential, but that other things are not essential? Why don't you get rid of that? Why don't you quit feeling that way about it? Who are you to put yourself up before God and the will of God and say, "Some things are essential because I like them, and other things are not because I don't like them"? Why don't you tonight believe in the Lord with all of your heart, turn away from sin, confess Christ before men, be buried in baptism for the remission of sins, arise to walk the new life, and walk the new life faithfully as long as God lets you live. Then BE a Christian after you have become one. Worship faithfully. That is the spirit of Christ. Worship regularly and serve him diligently. That is the spirit of Christ. If you haven't been doing this, then get right with him tonight, while together we stand and sing.

WHAT THE CHURCH NEEDS

I want to join Brother Phillips in expressing my appreciation for your presence tonight, and to say that we are glad to have all of you here. We especially appreciate the presence of the people from Largo who have seen fit to discontinue their Wednesday evening service in order to be with us. We hope that you will also heed his suggestion that if you have any questions that you would like to ask, I promise to do my best to give you a scriptural answer or to help you in any way that I may be able with any problem that may be troubling you. It is my ambition to preach the gospel of our Lord Jesus Christ, present it in its fulness, and to teach only the truth as God has revealed it. There is no good to be accomplished by presenting error or by teaching error, and if I do so, I do so unwittingly, not knowing what I'm doing and I would be glad to know that which I may present which is not in harmony with God's will.

Tonight we are speaking on the subject: *What the Church Needs*. As a background that I want to hold before you throughout this sermon tonight, I want to read a portion of the 4th chapter of Paul's letter to the church at Philippi, reading verses 8 and 9, and then verse 19 of the 4th chapter. He says: "Finally, brethren, whatsoever things are honorable, whatsoever things are just, whatsoever things are pure, whatsoever things are lovely, whatsoever things are of good report; if there be any virtue, and if there be any praise, think on these things. The things which ye both learned and received and heard and saw in me, these things do: and the God of peace shall be with you." "And my God shall supply every need of yours according to his riches in glory in Christ Jesus. Now unto our God and Father be the glory for ever and ever. Amen."

Those passages, friends, at least the concluding ones, with the summation of the thoughts contained in them with the statement that "God will supply every need," present the point that I want to call to your attention tonight. Paul is writing to the church at Philippi, a most wonderful congregation. He has attempted in this epistle to show them the things that they are to think about. His concluding remarks in the paragraph, a portion of which I just read for you, display such an ambition. Paul wants them to think on the things of God, the things of the Lord. He wants them to understand and to appreciate that which God wanted them to do. Now then he adds in conclusion that "God will supply every need." I think we can profit by thinking about that for a little while tonight: that God will supply the need of the church today, or even the non-Christian for that matter. God will supply his need. Well, what is his need? He needs to become a Christian. God supplies or provides the information that he needs in becoming a child of God. We will talk about that a little bit further along this evening. But God supplies the need of man—all men—and that is the principle that I want to refer you to tonight.

Now, of course, we understand that the church needs some things, and I think that is true almost everywhere you go. I believe we could say that the church is in need of some things. Well, what do we need? One of the first things I think we need is to learn the fact that we don't need some things. For instance, I'm looking at a passage of Scripture in Galatians the 1st chapter and verse 8. The writer says: "But though we, or an angel from heaven, preach any other gospel unto you than that which we have preached unto you, let him be accursed." And then he says: "As we said before, so say I now again, If any man preach any other gospel unto you than that ye have received, let him be accursed." Now here is the point: I think the church needs to recognize, first of all, the fact that she doesn't need new laws.

When the Lord Jesus Christ died on the cross, and when the Lord said, "It is finished," the Holy Spirit still had much work to do, but the polity and policy of the plan that God had in mind for the church, and the work of the

Lord in everything up to that time, was over. From then on the laws to govern the church were given by the Holy Spirit as the New Testament was written. From that time until now, and as long as man shall live, the church doesn't need any new laws.

I want you to notice a statement that he makes again in II Timothy the 3rd chapter, verses 16 and 17: "All scripture is given by inspiration of God, and is profitable for doctrine, for reproof, for correction, for instruction in righteousness: that the man of God may be perfect, thoroughly furnished unto all good works." The Scriptures are sufficient! We don't need some new revelation! It is not necessary for men to attempt to get new revelation from God because all Scripture that God has provided is profitable in order that the man of God may be perfect, completely furnished unto all good works. And then there is a statement in the last part of the Bible, in the book of John—II John the 9th chapter, which says: "Whosoever transgresseth, and abideth not in the doctrine of Christ, hath not God." You can't go beyond that which God has revealed. My point is that the church doesn't need new laws. The church doesn't need any laws in addition to the laws God has given us in His Word.

Now here is something else the church doesn't need. I don't think the church needs entertainment. You know, we have a rather strained idea about what it will take to pull people into the church. If you pull people into the church, so to speak, by entertaining them, then you would have to keep it up to keep them in the church, if you got them in that way. That is not what the church is for, my friends. People understand that, as a rule, preachers are rather poor entertainers. Why Bob Hope can beat nearly any preacher that I ever heard in my life cracking jokes. And I don't mean that I agree with all the jokes that Bob Hope cracks, although I don't think I ever heard him use any of the smutty things that sometimes you do hear. Maybe you have. That is not the point. The point is that preachers are rather inefficient with respect to matters along that line, and I think the church goes out of its way when it attempts to put on a big show for the people. Suppose you got them out to listen to the **Twin City Four** as they sing a quartet number, or to hear Mrs. Bla Bla sing a solo? I wonder what real good, so far as God's divine will is concerned, would they receive. The church doesn't need entertainment.

Now then you get a good grip on your seat. I want to make another statement: I don't think the church of the Living God needs to be popular! Respected? Yes. We want the respect of all earnest, honest, sincere men and women in a community. But so far as catering to the popular opinions of men and the popular side of society of a given locality, the church must not. When the church of the Living God degenerates to the point that it is seeking, through its membership, its preacher or some of the influential members of the church, to elevate the church that was purchased by the blood of the Lord Jesus Christ to a position of popularity by social climbing, we are using the wrong means. That is one of the things the church doesn't need.

I think I could go on and discuss these things, but I believe your minds are clear with regard to what we really want to say. What does the church need then? In Acts 2:42, after Peter had preached that memorable sermon on the day of Pentecost, the people cried out and said, "Men and brethren, what shall we do?" After Peter told them that by wicked hands they had crucified and slain the Lord, he said: "Repent, and be baptized every one of you in the name of Jesus Christ for the remission of sins, and ye shall receive the gift of the Holy Ghost. For the promise is unto you, and to your children, and to all that are afar off, even as many as the Lord our God shall call." Now watch verse 41, because that is the verse I want you to get. "Then they that gladly received his word were baptized: and the same day there were added unto them about three thousand souls." My thought is built on the word "received." I think one of the things the church needed then, and the church needs today, is a converted, preaching membership. This passage says: "Then they that gladly received his word were baptized: and the same day there were added unto them about three thousand souls." There are three thousand men and women who have obeyed the gospel of the Lord Jesus Christ and become the church in operation in the city of Jerusalem.

In the 4th chapter of the book of Acts and verse 4, the writer says, "Howbeit many of them which heard the word believed; and the number of the men was about five thousand." Three thousand on the day of Pentecost; over here in chapter 4 it has increased to five thousand. Now I turn the page and I read chapter 8—the 4th verse of chapter 8. It states that after Stephen had been put to death the church was persecuted. Saul of Tarsus was doing a great persecution against the church. And in the 4th verse of the 8th chapter: "Therefore they that were scattered abroad went every where preaching the word." They were scattered abroad except the apostles and these remained in the city of Jerusalem. Now my reasoning is this: after those people on the day of Pentecost obeyed the gospel, after they had been subjected to a severe persecution, having been indoctrinated in the truths of God by these capable men who taught them the way of the Lord, they were driven out of the city of Jerusalem. Well, did they quit? No. Did they quit talking about this great thing that had happened? No, sir. They went everywhere preaching the word.

You know, I think that is one of the needs of the church today. I think we need men and women in the church who will receive the word into their hearts. Of course, only those who received it were baptized for only those could be. Only those who were willing to do God's will could be baptized. You can change a man from the outside and sometimes make him do something that you would like for him to do, but he never amounts to the snap of your finger till you change him on the inside. You have got to change him inside. These people were changed in heart and in soul. They received the word. And when they received it into their hearts, they loved it so much, they believed it so strongly that they wanted other people to become the recipients of that same blessing that they had enjoyed and were enjoying. Hence, they went every where preaching the word. I just think we need that kind of people in the church today. I think I could say that is one of the greatest needs of the church today. Men and women hear the gospel, believe it and obey it, and I believe they become Christians all right, but I wonder to what extent they have received God's divine word. Friends, we are growing up in the church today, many of us, with the idea that the church doesn't amount to so much. We have just accepted what was presented to us and there has been no real scramble for it. We haven't had to exert much effort. And because of that we are not quite as active as we once were. I just want to say to you that the church of the Lord Jesus Christ has had to fight for every inch of ground that she has ever made up to the present time, and when we develop a membership that ceases to fight for the truths of God's divine will, we are going to stop gaining ground. The church, therefore, needs a militant membership that believes what the Bible teaches so strongly that we are ready to contend earnestly for the faith once for all delivered to the saints, that we are anxious to live and to practice the truth against all the forces of evil that may be about us. This nonchalant attitude that sometimes people have is damaging to the cause, and will not build up the work of the Lord in any community. Now, I believe that we are pretty well converted, for instance, on the idea of what we call first principles. For instance, take the matter of faith, and repentance, and confession and baptism. I think we understand those things. I can ask almost any member of the church: "Do you believe that an individual ought to obey the gospel according to the principles laid down in Acts the 8th chapter, where this man heard the gospel, believed it and obeyed it? Do you believe he ought to do what the people did on the day of Pentecost?"

"Yes, sir."

We are pretty well converted on those things. Take the name of God's people. The Bible tells us that the name of God's people is "Christian." There is no authority for the denominational names that people wear, that are divisive in nature. I think all understand that. That is not hard to get people to see. Acts the 11th chapter, verse 26, Acts 26:28; I Peter 4:16 use the name Christian. And the church is referred to as the *church*. In Acts the 2nd chapter and the 47th verse, the Lord added to the church daily those that were being saved. The Bible says that the kingdom is the church. Jesus, in speaking to the disciples, said, "Upon this rock I will build my church." And then he said, "I will give you the keys of the kingdom," almost in the same breath. We believe that the church of God is a correct name for that institution. Paul referred to it as the *church of the Lord* when he said to the elders "feed the church of the Lord which he purchased with his own blood." And so we don't have much difficulty with that. The same is true regarding the Lord's Supper. Ask most of the members of the church: "Do you think we ought to have the Lord's Supper on the Lord's day?"

"Yes, sir."

Most of us will contend for that. But what about the idea of regularity in worship? Suppose I were to write down here on the blackboard: "Members of the church ought to be regular in worship." "Well, I think we ought to go to church on Sunday morning, take the Lord's Supper and drop in a little contribution, but it is not necessary that we go Sunday night and Wednesday night, and pay any special attention to the meetings and things of that sort," they would say. Now I want to ask you, do you think the church as a whole is converted truly and is preaching truly the principles with regard to regularity in attendance?

And what about the subject of giving? Is every member of the church, shall I say, converted on the idea of giving of their means? There are members of the church who are going to be lost as certain as God is in His heaven, simply because of the fact that they are being stingy with the Lord, not giving of their means as they ought to give. Now how do I know that? I simply know that, as the Lord said, "by their fruits ye shall know them." I talk to some of the members of the church, and individuals, that could give many, many, many times as much to the Cause of the Lord as they are giving, but are giving only a small token of the amount of their income as they have been prospered. It is based upon your prosperity. A fellow said to me today with regard to an individual that had made a substantial contribution, "I think the reason that individual did it was only because he could take it off his income tax." Now that may be true, I don't know whether it is or not, but I just wonder if people are truly converted on giving. Don't you see the point, my brethren and friends? What does the church need? A converted, preaching membership; a membership that is converted to all these things.

What about personal purity? Listen to this passage: "Keep thyself pure." Do we need to convert the members of the church on such principles as that? In other words, does the church need to restudy that question the same as the question of giving, the same as the question of loyalty to the church and faithfulness with respect to attendance to the services of the Lord? What about the passage, "Visit the fatherless and widows in their afflictions, and keep one's self unspotted from the world?" You know, all these represent sermons within themselves, no doubt, but certainly they do represent things we ought to think about. The church is converted on some things. Yes, we believe in faith, repentance, confession and baptism—I would be the last fellow in the world to say that we ought not to emphasize those things; I believe them too. But, bless your soul, I think we ought to be converted on the subject of giving of our means. I think we ought to be converted on the subject of personal purity—purity of life.

But I pass on to another thought, and this is a second thing I think the church needs. I think the church needs a stronger and more faithful leadership or eldership that is more ambitious in applying themselves to their task as leaders and elders in the church of the Living God. I want to read a passage of Scripture for you, in the 20th chapter of Acts and the 17th verse, beginning, and then skipping over to the 28th verse. Paul called the elders of the church at Ephesus down to Miletus, the 17th verse tells us, and then in verse 28, he said to these men just before he was getting into the ship to bid them goodbye. He said: "Take heed therefore unto yourselves, and to all the flock, over which the Holy Ghost hath made you overseers, to feed the church of God, which he hath purchased with his own blood." Now let me break that down into its different parts. "Take heed unto yourselves," elders of the church, deacons of the church. I am going still further than that. I think that can be applied to the teachers in the Sunday school; the people who are taking the lead in the work of the Lord, "take heed unto yourselves." Then he said further to these elders, "Take heed to the flock." That is to the church. I believe there is a responsibility there. I think the church needs active elders, elders that will "eld," so to speak, if I could use such an expression. And deacons that will "deak," so to speak. I believe that is necessary. It is one of the needs of the church. And then Paul goes on and says, "Feed the church." Notice the three statements: "Take heed to yourselves; take heed to the flock; feed the church of God." They are to act as overseers or superintendents of the flock of God.

We have some splendid elders in this part of the state. I think I know the elders at Clearwater pretty well. They are, in my estimation, Godly, consecrated men who are doing a splendid job in that which God wants elders to do. I think we have one of the finest groups of men at Howard Avenue that it has ever been my privilege to work with, elders of the church who are zealous and conscientious, consecrated, pure and holy in life and in teaching. And that is necessary.

My friends, I think maybe where we are falling down on the job is that we are failing to inspire young men to want to become elders in the church, and to inspire them to grow up to be leaders over God's flock, and that is my reason for saying that we need consecrated, devout and active elders in the church of God today. One of the reasons why that some of the churches are having trouble is because they don't have a consecrated and devout leadership and eldership. And when I use that word **leadership,** I mean eldership. I don't mean a setup, called **leadership** that is to take the place of the elders. I don't believe there is such an organization as that taught in the Bible, but I believe that the elders are leaders, and that is what I mean when I say **leaders.** My friends, the elders are the ones who guard the flock, who guard the pulpit. They are to be strong, know the doctrine, and stand for the truth. And the church should develop young men to take the places of these who are rapidly getting older in the work, and doubtless, as the years go by we may not have the men to supply the places of these gallant soldiers of God. So I say the church needs elders who will oversee the work of the Lord.

Elders are a great encouragement to young men and women, depending on how successful they are in doing the work that God wants them to do. I remember a few years ago, I had not been preaching but a short time, and I was engaged in one of the first meetings that I ever preached in. In fact, I had never held any meetings. I had just been preaching on Sundays and didn't really know much about it, but I was in there doing the best I could. Well, Sunday morning I preached to a fairly large crowd of people. It was way back in the country. It was a small building, but that night when I went up to the church house, the building was literally packed and jammed. It made me feel pretty good. I thought, well, these people have come out to hear me. Of course they had not, but it made me feel good anyhow. And so as I came up—people were standing outside of the windows looking in—one of the elders came out to meet me as I came in. He is a wonderful man; one of the best friends I've got in this world, and I am sure he has forgotten the incident, and if he ever hears about this, doubtless, he will remember it. But anyhow it is so and I am going to tell it. Of course I was a young man and he was several years older than I and he thought maybe he would give me some good advice. He said, "Brother Pickup, you are going to have to be mighty careful in your sermon tonight you know?"

I said, "Yes, I am always careful in my sermons, at least I want to be."

"Well, now," he said, "you want to be mighty careful tonight because the house is full of Methodists, and we want to be sure that we do not offend any of our Methodist neighbors because they might not come back."

You know, friends, I never do offend anybody. You can bring your Methodist friends, your Baptist friends, your Presbyterian friends, your Roman Catholic neighbors, you can bring anybody; I will never offend a single one of them —not one. Now if the gospel of the Lord Jesus Christ offends them, I am not responsible. I am going to preach the truth and I am going to show what error is. And I am going to show why it is. Of course, sometimes people get their feelings hurt a little bit, but not much. They come back. And so, of course, when that brother said that to me, I just didn't know what to do. I had not been preaching very long and I didn't know nearly as much about it as I learned a little bit later. I went on into the church building and I sat down there, you know, and went over my sermon notes. I had them there with me, you know, and I went over them a little bit to see if I could fix the thing up so I would not offend anybody. Finally I got up in the pulpit and evidently did a fairly respectable job. The people went out of the building that night and pumped my hand, "Wonderful sermon, young man, wonderful sermon."

I felt pretty good about it. And they came back Monday night. A big crowd of people on Monday night. I preached another sermon about like the one I preached Sunday night. There wasn't much to it, but it kept them coming. I told a few jokes and told a few graveyard yarns and had them crying and they thought it was a wonderful sermon, and I did too. Tuesday night the same thing. I preached on love. I had not been married long enough to know much about love then. I preached on first one thing and another, you know, that would be perfectly acceptable to anybody, and the people thought I was the greatest preacher that ever came in that community. "Greatest man ever been here," they would say. My, I was all swelled up and felt good! I can just see this elder now; he smiled about that thing. He was as pleased as a kitten over a bowl of milk. We just had the biggest time you ever saw. But there was one thing wrong, and it didn't take me but a few nights to see what it was: there was nobody sitting on the front bench when the invitation song was sung. I had not told them what to do to be saved. I had sort of tickled their ears with a few little stories and things like that, but I didn't get down to real preaching. The song leader, Brother Tom Nicks, one of the best friends I have, and a man who has meant a lot to me in my preaching, came to me about it. He and I have since then worked together in many meetings in hard places and in many sections of the country. He came to me after about Wednesday night and said: "Harry, what in the world has gotten into you? What is the matter? Why don't you break down on some of those good old sermons that you used to preach out at the State Prison (Nashville, Tennessee)? You can preach if you will. How about "The Name of God's People," or the "Conversion of the Ethiopean Eunuch?" I said, "That is exactly what I am going to do."

That is exactly what I did. I started in right then. By Sunday night of the second week they began to come down the aisle, one or two at a time, you know. Before that meeting was over we had baptized about 25 people.

I went back the next year, right in the same place, and we baptized 18 or 20 more. The third year in the same spot we had about the same number of additions; somewhere in the neighborhood of 60 people and I suppose half of them were Methodists. That elder had said to me, "Brother Pickup, by all means don't offend the Methodists," and I didn't; but we sure did lead a whole lot of them to Christ. I go back there for a meeting in 1954, I was there this past summer in the same spot. Some of the same people that obeyed the gospel in that first meeting are still living in that community. They are influential members of the body of Christ, leaders in the community and doing a great work for the Lord. The only reason that they are is because of the fact that the song leader got hold of the preacher and said, "Son, preach the gospel and quit telling deathbed stories."

The point is this: we need elders that know the difference between truth and error, and will take young preachers and old preachers or anybody else and say, "Look here, bud, you shell it down like God teaches it in His Word and tell people what to do to be saved. Tell them what the church is. Tell them what God wants men to do in living the Christian life. Expose sin and error, both in the church and out of it. Let people know what God wants men to do." There will be a lot of people who will obey the gospel, and in the final analysis of all things, a lot more names inscribed on the Lamb's book of life. That is a need of the church.

But I want to notice another statement. I am looking at Romans I and verse 8. I think the church needs more loyalty and devotion on the part of all the members of the church. Yes, we need a strong, active, preaching membership. We need a strong, active, zealous eldership. We need more loyalty and devotion on the part of everybody. We can stand a whole lot of that in the state of Florida, if I know anything about the work, and I think I do. I have traveled all over the state of Florida. I don't know how many places I have been, but I have been in most of the localities of this state. Listen to this: "I thank my God through Jesus Christ for you all." (That's a good old southern expression that Paul uses here). "I thank my God through Jesus Christ for you all, that your faith is spoken of throughout the whole world." Over here in Revelation the 2nd chapter and verse 10 John says: "Be thou faithful unto death and I will give thee a crown of life." What is that? Loyalty and devotion. God wants men and women in the church who are loyal, who are devoted to the principles of right and faithfulness. And when individuals have that, then God will bless them because of it.

In Acts the 2nd chapter and verse 42 the writer says: "And they continued steadfastly in the aspostles' doctrine and fellowship, and in breaking of bread, and in prayers." They continued in:

Number one: The apostles' doctrine.

Number two: In fellowship.

Number three: In breaking of bread (that's the Lord's Supper).

Number four: In prayers.

Now what were they doing? Standing fast—steadfast for the truth. That's loyalty and devotion. Some years ago you made a promise to your wife or your husband. One of the things the preacher asked you is if you would stand by that companion in sickness and in health, forsaking all others for that one, and that one alone. That is loyalty and devotion. God wants men and women in the church who are steadfast and who are loyal to the principles of truth as taught in God's divine word.

But there is one other point that I want you to notice and that is based upon a statement that is made over here in the 1st chapter of the book of James, and beginning with about verse 22 and reading through 25. He says: "But be ye doers of the word, and not hearers only, deceiving your own selves. For if any be a hearer of the word, and not a doer, he is like unto a man beholding his natural face in a glass: for he beholdeth himself, and goeth his

way, and straightway forgetteth what manner of man he
was." Now watch. "But whoso looketh into the perfect
law of liberty, and continueth therein, he being not a for-
getful hearer, but a doer of the work, this man shall be
blessed in his deed." I think we need more vision in the
church. What do you mean vision? Vision to look within
the hearts and lives of us all and see what's wrong with
us. Can you do that? Have you got the nerve, my friend,
my brother, to look into your heart and say: "What is
wrong with me?" We go to the doctor and tell him what's
wrong with us, or at least answer his questions. And we
tell him that this or that or the other is wrong with us
and finally he writes out a prescription and he says, "My
diagnosis is this because from what you have told me I
think that perhaps this is the one thing that is the matter
with you." It reminds me of the sick man who said, "I
want you to bring me a horse doctor." Somebody asked,
"Why in the world do you want a horse doctor?" He said,
"The horse doctor can't ask the patient any questions, so
he has got to be right." The diagnosis is based upon what
the doctor really KNOWS about horse ailments. Now here
is my point: I believe it isn't a question of my answering
or asking any questions with respect to God, but rather
a willingness to look into the perfect law of liberty and
answer the questions based upon what that law directs me
to do.

Have I got the vision to do that? You know, I can see
your sins without any trouble. I can see your mistakes.
Of course I don't make any myself, but I can see the ones
you make. But the thing I need, and the thing all of us
in the church need, is to be able to look into our own hearts
and say, "What's wrong with me?" That is one of the
things that is wrong with so many people today; they can
not stand to make an observation of themselves in the light
of God's divine will. We are prone to pitch the thing over
our shoulders to somebody else and say, "Well, I don't think
I need that; that's for this fellow or that fellow," when
in reality the thing really and truly is meant for us. I

have had people to come to me in years past, after I had preached a sermon directly dealing with some particular sin that I hoped that I could get them to see they were guilty of, and as they would go out of the building they would say, "Brother Pickup, you were talking right to me tonight." I would say, "Aw, No, I did not really have you in mind." Of course, all the time I did, but I didn't want to hurt their feelings. But I don't do that any more. When somebody says to me, "Looks like to me you were preaching right squarely to me tonight," I say, "Buddy, I'm glad you got the point. You are exactly right, I was preaching right to you." Now I think we ought to be willing to accept such instruction. You and I ought to have the vision to see what is wrong with us.

But let us take it a little further than that. I think the church at Clearwater or Largo or Howard Avenue or anywhere else needs to have the vision to see what is wrong with IT as a church. Sometimes there is something wrong with us that we would discover if we would only investigtae. That is a certain cautiousness which should characterize the members, the elders, the preacher, the deacons and all concerned with the work of the Lord. I would say that those who are conscientiously trying to correct those things that are wrong will find that the church will remain in a state of peace and tranquility over a longer period of time because of that watchfulness. Therefore, the church needs vision, vision to look within itself. I need vision to look at myself. I am prone to say the mistake is made by the other fellow rather than by myself. Now that is one kind of vision. The other kind of vision is that about which the Lord spoke to his disciples on one occasion when he said: "Lift up your eyes and look on the fields that are white already unto harvest." I think the church needs vision to see the need of preaching the gospel and leading souls to Christ in its own community, and beyond the borders of its own community.

To recapitulate, friends, the church needs a strong, preaching membership. The church needs a strong, active eldership. The church needs loyalty and devotion. The church needs to consider the matters with respect to its own self in the faithfulness and loyalty of its own members. The church of God today needs vision. The kind of vision that can look at the sins within, at the opportunities within, and the things that are without, as we plan to teach the gospel of Christ beyond the borders of its own influence in its immediate locality. These are some of the things the church needs.

Now, friends, if you can appreciate and understand that YOU fit into this program, let me ask you tonight in conclusion: What is your individual need? If you are not a Christian, you need to obey the gospel of the Lord Jesus Christ. You can't be saved without obeying the gospel of the Lord Jesus Christ. Jesus taught that men needed to have the gospel preached to them, and so he told the apostles to go out and preach it to every nation. You can be stubborn and hard-headed about it if you want to, but one day you are going to stand before God in the judgment—and I'm going to talk about the judgment during this meeting —you are going to stand before God in the judgment to give an account for the way that you have misused your opportunities, or neglected to do his will. So, if you are not a Christian, let me urge you tonight to believe in the Lord with all of your heart, to turn away from every sin, to confess Christ before men, to be buried in baptism for the remission of your sins and then rise to walk the new life and be faithful and loyal and zealous in doing His will. If you are out of duty, if you have been cold and careless and negligent and indifferent, or if you have sinned publicly and need to make a public confession of those sins, we hope that tonight you will do that. Confess your faults one to another, pray one for another that you may be healed. If you are here tonight and a subject of the invitation, will you come while together we stand and sing the **song**?

SEEING THE DIFFERENCE

I want to say that I am happy to be here tonight and to have a part with you in this service. We trust that all of us may recognize our responsibilities and obligations with regard to our duty to God. I try to be conscious of my responsibilities and obligations. I never stand on my feet before an audience to preach to them God's eternal truths unless I have previously prayed to God to guide me and direct me in teaching the truth as God would have me to present it. But I want to suggest to you, friends, that responsibilitity does not rest alone with me, but with you as well. While the preacher must stand before God and give an account for the way he preaches the gospel, or fails to preach it, the people who listen likewise must one day give an account for the manner in which they hear and heed, or disregard, God's divine will. The meeting, therefore, is being conducted with this in mind, that all of us may learn what we can about the Lord and his teaching for us, and that we may be persuaded to change our ways, if change our ways we need to do.

We suggested that we would be glad to answer questions, and we will do the best we can with all of them. If we can't answer then, we will just say so. We have one question tonight. The first part of it says: "What about death-bed confessions?" And the second part: "What about praying for those dead and buried?"

Now usually most of the questions we receive have to deal with things that we usually discuss in a sermon, but not always. So because we may not get to these in this meeting, I want to take the time now just to spend a few minutes in giving what I consider to be a scriptural answer to both of these questions. Now the first one: "What about death-bed confessions?" I am assuming that the party has in mind simply a confession of their faith in the Lord and then, without any further obedience to God, dying in that condition. That would be a death-bed confession. Well, the Bible teaches that confession is im-

portant; that we must confess Christ before men. In the
10th chapter of Matthew, Jesus said: "Everyone therefore who shall confess me before men, him will I also confess before my Father who is in heaven. But whosoever
shall deny me before men, him will I also deny before my
Father who is in heaven." Now confession is important,
but is that all there is to it? No, friends, of course not,
and you understand that. There is much more to it than
simply saying, "I believe in the Lord." The Bible says
the devils believe and tremble. So the fact that a person
would say, "I believe," and that's all, wouldn't necessarily
mean that he had done that part of his duty which he
could have done, even on that occasion. The thought that
I have in mind, and the answer to this, is that God demands complete obedience. It doesn't make any difference
whether the person has waited until he is about ready to
die, or whether he does it at some other time in life. People seem to think that the approach of death gives dignity
to the conduct of that person's life, but it doesn't. It
doesn't make any difference whether the person is doing
this just immediately before death or ten years before
death, God rquires the same things of him. It isn't a question of being able to make a death-bed confession just
before death and have God say, "Come on in," anymore
than God would say that if it were done ten years before
death. Death does not lend any special dignity to a person's life, my friends, the matter is a question of obedience,
and Jesus became the author of eternal salvation unto all
them that obey him. One of the things that people need
to do is to obey. Well, obedience consists of several things,
not only confession of Christ before men—that is one
thing—but he must repent of his sins, he must turn
away. "The times of this ignorance God winked at; but
now commandeth all men every where to repent." So the
person must not only confess that he believes in the Lord,
or confess Christ, but there has got to be a state of genuine repentance in his life. Not only is that true, but
that individual must be baptized for the remission of sins,

for the Bible says that you must be baptized in order to receive the blessings of eternal life. It was Jesus himself who said: "He that believeth and is baptized shall be saved." So salvation is predicated, not simply upon a confession, not only upon repentance, not even upon both of them. In order to be a Christian one must believe in the Lord, have faith in Christ, he must confess Christ before men, having repented of his sins, and he must also be baptized for the remission of sins. The point I want you to see is that it doesn't matter whether the individual is about to die or is ten years from death. The approach of death lends no dignity of his position or mitigate the requirements God has laid down in His word for him to do. If it did, then you could see that there would be many laws of pardon, and God would be a respecter of persons. All you would have to do, even though you lived for the devil all your life, would be to make a death-bed confession and all would be well. The Bible teaches that God is no respecter of persons, and of course that wouldn't do.

Now the second question: "What about praying for these dead and buried?" Well, once again I want to read a passage of scripture. The Bible says, "All Scripture is given by inspiration of God and is profitable to teach, to reprove, to correct, to instruct in justice, that the man of God may be perfect, furnished to every good work." Incidentally, this is a Catholic version that I am using. This particular Bible that I hold in my hand has the imprimatur of the pope of Rome on it, the Rev. William H. McClellen, S. J. and with Pope Leo's imprimatur on it. I mention that because I want you to know that the use of different translations makes little or no difference. Catholics believe in prayers for the dead, so I am using their version.

Now the Bible says the scriptures inspired of God are profitable. Profitable for what? Well, for teaching, in order to correct, and to reprove and to instruct men in the things that God would have them to do. Well why that? I'll tell you. The Bible teaches that men, while they live, are to be the recipients of the blessings of God and we are to pray for the living. There is not a single example in all the Bible from beginning to end of praying for the dead. It has always been a strange thing to me why people would want to do this when God's Word is silent with respect to it. The Bible says nothing about praying for the dead. My answer would be this: If the Holy Scriptures furnish us unto all good works, then I have got to proceed to the scriptures to find out where that is so or where the Book teaches it. But it doesn't; therefore, on the basis of the silence of the scriptures I must of necessity refrain from praying for the dead.

I'll tell you something else: you can't change the state of the dead. The Bible says that every man must appear before the judgment seat of Christ. The Bible also says that it is appointed unto man once to die, and after death, the judgment. So as man dies, that is the way he is going to come into the judgment. Now I will tell you, friends, you can just pray all you want to over the dead; you can heap flowers as high as this building, and you can sing the sweetest songs in Zion, but you can't change the state of the dead. If so, God has not revealed it. There is nothing under heaven that man can do to change the state of the dead, if this Bible is so, and I believe that it is. I know God's word is true with regard to such matters, and the Bible teaches that prayers are to be said for people who are living. And so we pray. Let me give you some of the passages of Scripture. "Pray without ceasing." "By supplication let your wants be known unto God.' We have the record of the Lord Jesus Christ teaching his disciples to pray, and he told them to pray for the things they desired. Thus by prayer we make our wants known unto God. The church prayed for Peter when he was put in prison. We pray for the saints who are sick, those who are in need and all who may need our prayers. But after death comes, there is no reason to pray for the change of that person's condition, because these passages which I have read state very clearly that as man dies that's the way he is coming into the judgment. I hope this is clear and that maybe good has resulted from the study of these things.

Now tonight I want to talk about the subject, *Seeing The Difference.* What do we mean by *Seeing The Difference?* I have a scripture that I want to read for you from the Old Testament. It is in the 3rd chapter of the book of I Kings, beginning at verse 5. "In Gibeon the Lord appeared to Solomon in a dream by night: and God said, Ask what I shall give thee. And Solomon said, Thou hast shewed unto thy servant David my father great mercy, according as he walked before thee in truth, and in righteousness, and in uprightness of heart with thee; and thou hast kept for him this great kindness, that thou hast given him a son to sit on his throne, as it is this day. And now, O Lord my God, thou hast made thy servant king instead of David my father: and I am but a little child: I know not how to go out or come in. And thy servant is in the midst of thy people which thou hast chosen, a great people, that cannot be numbered not counted for multitude. Give therefore thy servant an understanding heart to judge thy people, that I may discern between good and bad: for who is able to judge this thy so great a people? And the speech pleased the Lord, that Solomon had asked this thing."

One of the things in the mind of the great man, and he was the wisest man that we know anything about, was the fact that he wanted to know the difference. Lots of people today say, "Well, I think it is important in some things but in others it is not." Why, friends, in nearly everything it is important to know the difference, and especially in matters that concern how we live, where we will go after we die and all matters that effect either our present or our eternal destiny.

I heard of a fellow over here in Alabama some few years ago that was making a lot of money counterfeiting. He would take a ten dollar bill, tear off the opposite corners, or cut them off nicely, then he would take a one dollar bill and tear off all four of the corners and match the ten's on the opposite corners of the one dollar bills—the ones he had cut off the tens. He then had two pretty good ten dollar bills with the number of corners on it that the law required: namely, two. He passed a lot of those ten dollar bills which were made of the ones. He made quite a little bit on it until they caught up with him. We have various and sundry kinds of forgery that is going on today. I even got in the papers over in Tampa just a few weeks ago, right about Christmas time. Some fellow was forging my name. I went up to see the checks and gave them my signature. I said, "This is not my signature." and they said, "We can see that." The people who cashed those checks didn't know the difference between a check that was good and a check that was bad. Two of them were for $20.00 and two others were for $25.00. Some people are out $90.00 because they didn't know the difference. This could have been you. Of course in matters like that we want to know the difference between counterfeit money and genuine money. We wouldn't think of accepting something if we had the slightest doubt that it might be counterfeit.

Now I want to tell you, friends, you had better not accept a counterfeit religion. You had better be certain that you accept the real thing because if you don't know the difference, it may be that you will land in hell as a result of it. Well, why? I'll tell you. God has given us understanding and wisdom; He has given us minds with which to think, and the fellow who turns his thinking over to somebody else, especially in the field of Christianity, is making a terrible mistake. You need to think about the difference between certain things in religious matters. Many times you hear people say—and I've heard preachers say it—you don't need to especially bother about the difference; there is not any real difference, implying, at least, that it really doesn't make any difference what you do and how you live so long as you go ahead and do the best you can. God's word teaches otherwise than that, and I think you ought to know that which is right and that which is wrong with regard to the word of God the same as with regard to other matters.

Now, friends, I want you to notice some of the things we are going to talk about tonight under one particular heading, and that is the subject of authority. I am going to discuss the difference between the authority of man and the authority of Christ. First of all, I want you to notice a passage of scripture from the Old Testament that deals with this idea respecting the home. I think that you ought to know the difference between the thing that God has laid down as His authority in the home, and the authority of man as man executes his own authority with respect to his own ideas. You know, there is a lot of difference in the way we raise children from one generation to another. Why, I can remember the old fashioned method that was used with respect to my upbringing. My father was not a Christian but he had a marvelous way with children, and he believed that he ought to teach people, teach boys and girls in his home, what was parental authority. He didn't know it but he was following the teaching of God with respect to that matter. Let me read it for you. In Proverbs the 13th chapter and verse 24: "He that spareth his rod hateth his son: but he that loveth him chasteneth him betimes;" and then you remember it was the wise man Solomon who also said, "Train up the child in the way that he should go: and even when he is old, he will not depart from it."

But you know there came in some brand new ideas on child training and parental authority about 25 years ago. Soon after I started preaching (I wasn't supposed to know much about how to raise children) there were some people who would sorta wink at me, I mean wink their eyes or look down their noses, at the suggestions I made about rearing children. That was because I was just a young man then. My children were much younger than they are now, and a young man is not supposed to know. Why, friends, you don't have to be an old man with a lot of experience to tell people how to raise children, I mean to tell them correctly. I tell people about hell but I have never been there. A young man can tell people what to do to be saved the same as an old man. A young man can tell you how to raise your children the same as an old man, provided he follows the scriptures. Of course he may not have had any experience along that line, but what I am talking about tonight is not the experience of the preacher, be he young or old, but what does God say about the matter of parental authority in the home. God teaches that we must follow His way with respect to this, but somebody in the modern school says: "Yes, and if you do you will suppress the little fellow's spirit of self-expression." I say that may be right, but you may also raise a little rebel (and I like to have said *devil*, but of course that would never do to use such expressions, and yet actually that is about what it amount to).

My friends, my point is that: God's authority in the home must be respected. Sometimes wives don't understand what is the authority of God in the home. "Oh," they say, "Yes I do, I understand what God's authority is, but I am not especially inclined to bow my will to the will of the man that God has given to be with me." Now let me tell you this, The Bible says the husband is the head of the house, or the head of the wife, even as Christ is the head of the church and he is the Saviour of the body. The wife, therefore, is in subjection to the husband, which doesn't mean that he tramples her under his foot. You understand that. It doesn't mean that he is a tyrant, but he is a companion to his wife and she is a companion to him. There is a mutual obligation that runs all the way through.

I teach a course at Florida Christian College in *Home And Family*. I think it is one of the best courses they have in the whole college—of course, one reason is because I teach it and and naturally I would feel that way about my own course. We teach young people to respect exactly what God says concerning authority in the home. When a man becomes a tyrant and fails to follow the wisdom of the Lord in ruling his children and managing his affairs, then he violates God's authority the same as the wife does if she doesn't respect God's authority. When they in turn neglect their children and fail to rear them in the nuture and admonition of the Lord (Eph. 6:1-4), then we violate God's command and respect our own instead of the authority of God.

But I want to read another passage. This one concerns authority in the church. What does the Bible teach concerning authority in the church? Of course you know that the Bible IS the authority, and I'm going to get to that in a minute, but I'm talking about the authority with respect to the MANAGEMENT of the church. Listen to Acts 20:28: Paul said to the elders of the church at Ephesus when he called them down to Miletus, "Take heed therefore unto yourselves, and to all the flock, over the which the Holy Ghost hath made you overseers, to feed the church of God, which he hath purchased with his own blood." Where is the authority, therefore, that God has delegated in the church of the Living God? Why it is in the eldership, the men who have been appointed to the eldership to oversee the work—the superintendents of the flock of God. Now notice: they are to feed the church of the Living God, they are to direct the affairs of the church, and thus the authority with respect to the management of the church is delegated to the elders. Of course there is no appeal from divine authority, and I'm not speaking of that just yet, but I'm talking about God's authority in the church through the designated leaders, the elders of the family of God who are to oversee the work.

Now then, friends, we hasten on to still another thought that is the main idea that I want to get before you tonight, and that is the difference between the authority of Christ as the head of the church, and the authority of man. In the 5th chapter of the book of John and the 22nd verse this statement is made: "For the Father judgeth no man, but hath committed all judgment unto the Son." In the 17th chapter of Matthew and the 5th verse: "While he" (that is Peter) "yet spake, behold, a bright cloud over-shadowed them: and behold a voice out of the cloud, which said, This is my beloved Son, in whom I am well pleased; hear ye him." The authority, therefore, is in the Lord— the Lord Jesus Christ—so when I preach the gospel to you we must understand the difference between the authority of Christ and the authority of man with respect to the teachings and practices in which men engage. Now the elders are the superintendents of the flock, charged with the responsibility of feeding the flock—when they are distributing to the necessity of the saints in a spiritual sense —and directing and guiding the affairs of the congregation. Of course the spiritual food that they feed must be that which has the approval of Christ.

Well, the Book says that Christ is the authority, and I believe that most of us understand that. But let us notice another statement. In the 28th chapter of the book of Matthew, verses 18 and 20, Jesus said: "And Jesus came and spake unto them, saying, All power (authority) is given unto me in heaven and in earth. Go ye therefore, and teach all nations, baptizing them in the name of the Father, and of the Son, and of the Holy Ghost: teaching them to observe all things whatsoever I have commanded you: and, lo, I am with you always, even unto the end of the world." He is the authority, the Lord Jesus Christ is said to have ALL authority, so we write the word "ALL" up here on the blackboard because he himself said, "all authority both in heaven and on earth hath been given unto me."

Now, friends, how much is "all authority"? Well, every bit of it. There isn't any authority that man has with regard to the teaching of the Bible, it matters not what it is. If Christ has spoken on any subject, that is the end of the matter. If the apostles, the delegated authority, have spoken on the question, that is Christ speaking. When Peter speaks with regard to a matter, that is the voice of Christ or the voice of God. When Paul speaks that is the voice of God. When Matthew speaks, that is the voice of God. And thus we have the authority of the Lord.

When Jesus said, "All authority hath been given unto me," then he meant exactly that, but you watch the difference between the authority of Christ and the authority of man. Take for example the creed. What is a creed? Well, it comes from the Latin "credo" meaning "I believe" or "to believe," simply a statement of faith. We have prayer books and we have creeds of various denominational churches. The Methodists have a creed, the Presbyterians have a creed, the Episcopalians have a creed, the various denominations whose names you can call, most of them have certain little books that they call the creed book, and that creed book tells what they believe. Now then, suppose that this is not a song book which I hold in my hand, but a creed book (holds song book in hand). Here in the other hand I have the Word of God. This is what Peter says, what Paul says, what Christ says; here is what the Lord has said through the inspired apostles, but there (pointing to song book) is what I believe about the thing that God has said. Now you watch. Don't you see how that when I accept something that is other than the word of God, I am accepting something that takes FROM the authority of the Lord Jesus Christ? What effect does my conduct, therefore, have upon his authority if I do like that? I'll tell you by relating an incident which happened some years ago. I married a girl whose name was H-E-I-S-T—Heist. (Incidentally I am still married to her). On her father's side of the family the people were, most of them, Lutherans. Of course the name is a dead give-away being German to the core. Some years after we were married, we moved out in the eastern part of Nashville. One day a Lutheran preacher knocked on the door. My wife went to the door and he said to her: "Are you a member of the Heist family?"

She said: "Yes, I used to be. I married a Pickup, but my name used to be Heist."

Well, he had a little laugh about that, of course. He said: "Well, we are starting a new Lutheran church out here in this community and we thought you people would be interested in joining it, because we want to get the thing started off in a big way."

She said: "No, sir, I would not be interested in it because I am a Christian."

He said, "Oh I thought maybe you were, but we felt sure you would want to come over and be with us."

She said, "No, sir, I don't believe I do."

"Well," he said, "what church are you a member of, if you are not a member of the Luther church?" (He thought everybody that had a German name was Lutheran, but, of course, that is not so.)

She said: "I am a member of the church of Christ."

"The church of Christ," he said, "what is that like?"

She said, "It is the church of the New Testament."

"Oh, yes," he said, "I know what that is, the church of the New Testament. We all get our doctrines out of the New Testament, but what do you believe?"

She said, "We just believe the New Testament."

"You believe the New Testament? Yes, I know that." (He thought he was just using theological terms that she couldn't get.) So he tried again, "Yes, I know, but what I mean is what do you people practice, what do you believe?"

She said, "Why, we just believe and practice the teaching of the New Testament."

"Yes," he said, "Mrs. Pickup, I know that, but don't you have another little book somewhere that tells what you believe?"

She says, "Yes, we have got one that tells what we believe and it is the New Testament."

"Yes," he said, "but isn't there something else, isn't there something in ADDITION to the New Testament?"

She said, "No, sir, there is not."

And do you know, he was completely flabbergasted, if I could use that expression simply meaning that he had never heard of such a thing.

Now listen here, friends, can't I just be a child of God, a Christian, and not have something else other than the New Testament that tells what I believe or where I stand with regard to things? Can't I just have the New Testament? Why of course. Listen: the Bible says ALL authority is in Christ, therefore, I have every bit of it right here. (Pointing to the New Testament). I don't need something else in addition to this. What have I done with the Lord and his authority when I accept a human creed to tell what I believe? Somebody says, "Well, it is the same thing as the Bible." All right, if the creed that you follow is different from the Word of God—one single thing in it—then you had better not use it. If it is the same thing as the Word of God you don't need it: it is useless.

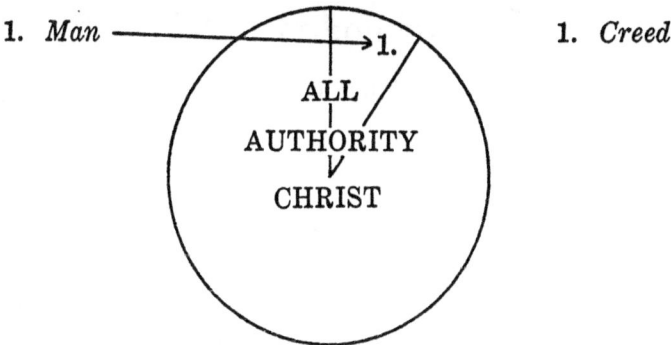

1. *Man* ——————— 1. *Creed*

ALL
AUTHORITY
CHRIST

My point is that it is a question of authority. I am going to let the Lord speak; I am going to let Him direct me, not through some idea or some human statement that has been made by a man or a group of men. I believe that God has written the Bible in such a way that intelligent people with ordinary understanding can open it and read it and can understand it. This is my reason for saying that if you have a creed—something in addition to what

God has given us in the New Testament—then you need
to know the difference between the authority of Christ and
the authority of man. Many people bow in submission to
the will of man by following traditions and creeds, most
of which are built on human interpretations that have
been handed down through the ages, following them in
preference to the principles of New Testament Christianity.

But I want you to notice still something else that I
think maybe we could think about for just a minute or
two. I am looking at a statement that I have jotted down
here on the margin of this Bible that is open, which concerns infant church membership. Let me write that down
up here on the blackboard. (Writes on blackboard: Infant
church membership).

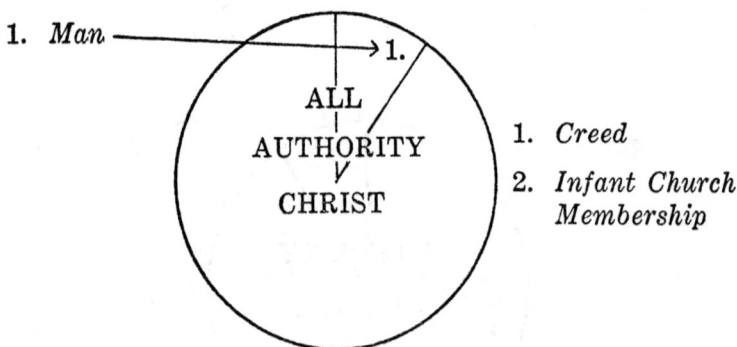

1. *Man* ——————

ALL
AUTHORITY
CHRIST

1. *Creed*
2. *Infant Church
   Membership*

What about babies in the church? Some people say it
is mighty nice. I knew a Presbyterian preacher, a wonderful fellow, who was talking to some of the members of the
church about infant church membership. He said he
knew there wasn't any Bible authority for it. Then somebody said, "Where do you go for your authority?"

"Oh, well, we go back to the law of the Old Testament;
the law which teaches circumcision for instance, beginning
with Abraham."

Well now over here on the blackboard we have *man*
as the authority for the creed, and now we write the

word *Abraham* as the authority for infant church membership.

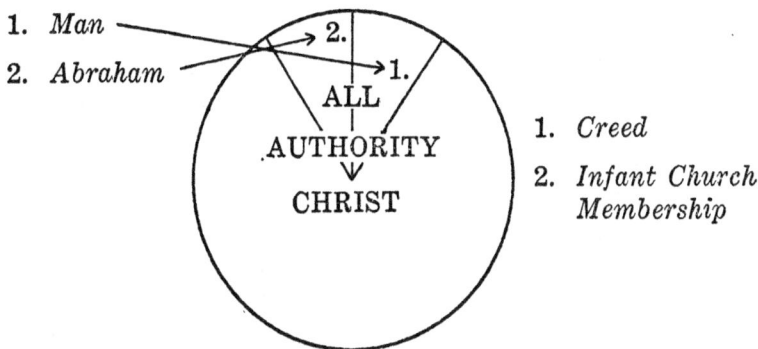

1. *Man*
2. *Abraham*

2.

1.

ALL

.AUTHORITY

CHRIST

1. *Creed*
2. *Infant Church Membership*

Have you not heard people say such things? The preacher I mentioned also said, "I know there is no authority for it, but the mothers get so much satisfaction out of it. It is a pleasant thing for them; they like to go through the ceremonies of dedicating their little babies and so we have infant church membership, but there really isn't any authority for it." Some of you who think there is authority for infant church membership may question that statement, but you look again and see that there is not one single solitary statement in all the New Testament about babies being members of the church. What do you suppose you could add to the soul of an innocent baby whose soul is far purer than your soul and mine until he reaches the age of accountability unto God? Why not a single solitary thing. Babies don't have to be saved; they are already safe, so far as their salvation is concerned. But some say, "Oh, but they had infants in the church back in the Old Testament regime, and so we go back to Abraham for authority." Well I thought we were going to take Christ as authority, and look what we have done now. We have taken out a slice of his authority for the creed and we have dedicated that to man—any man that writes a creed. Then we have to take out another slice over here on the ground of infant church membership, and we are going to have to give Abraham credit for that, because people say that Abraham is the father of circumcision which admitted infants under the Old law; hence, it will be all right to have babies in the church under the new law, in the church of the living God today. I'll tell you, friends, there is one thing wrong with all of this: God has not authorized it, the Bible gives no authority for it. If we are going to speak where the Bible speaks, if we are going to follow the inspired record, then we need to do only as it authorizes us. Only as we follow the Word of God can we be sure that we are doing the Lord's will. What does such as this do to the authority of Christ? Well, we have taken two pretty big chunks out of it, and I think you can see where even we may take out some more.

Suppose we look at the subject of sprinkling for baptism. What does the Book teach with regard to that? Not one single solitary thing! The Roman Catholic Church practices sprinkling for baptism, as do many of the other pedo-baptist organizations and it recognizes that God is not the authority for sprinkling. Ask a Catholic priest what about the authority for sprinkling, what does the Bible say on the subject, and he will tell you that the Bible does not authorize it. There is no statement in the Bible with regard to sprinkling. Catholic priests are intelligent, well educated men. They have a good knowledge of the original language, they know the meaning of the Greek, and they understand that the word that we translate "baptism" is really not translated at all but is anglicized. *Baptizo* is not a translated word, it is an anglicized word. What does it mean? It means "to dip or to plunge; to immerse." It doesn't mean to sprinkle. That is *rantizo*, a different word altogether. But you have seen this word as the Bible gives it, numerous times. For example Romans 6:4: "Therefore we are buried with him by baptism into death: that like as Christ was raised up from the dead by the glory of the Father, even so we also should walk in newness of life."

Well, where does the authority for sprinkling come

from? Where do Catholics and the Methodists and the Presbyterians and all the various denominations that are pedo-baptists get the authority for doing it? Well, it doesn't come from the word of God. It comes from a practice that has followed the tradition of the church. It does not come from God's divine will. Well, somebody says, "I read something in the Bible about Moses sprinkling the people when they were gathered at the foot of Mt. Sinai." Yes, we read in Exodus 24:3-8 how he sprinkled with blood the book of the covenant, the alter and the people of Israel. Also we learn that when the priest of the Old Testament went into the Holy of Holies, he didn't go in except with blood and that was sprinkled on the various articles of furniture, but that is not baptism in any sense of the word.

"Well, it sorta looks like it," somebody says.

No, friends, that is not baptism, that was the Old Testament ceremony of sprinkling the blood to bind a covenant God made with Israel. Clean water, that water which had been run through burnt ashes of a red heifer is mentioned as being "sprinkled" on idol worshippers in Ezekiel 36:25, but water, unmixed with anything, was never sprinkled upon anybody for anything under any covenant.

Somebody says, "Oh, yes, but I know Moses did that sprinkling back there." Well, all right. So we go back to Moses as authority for sprinkling.

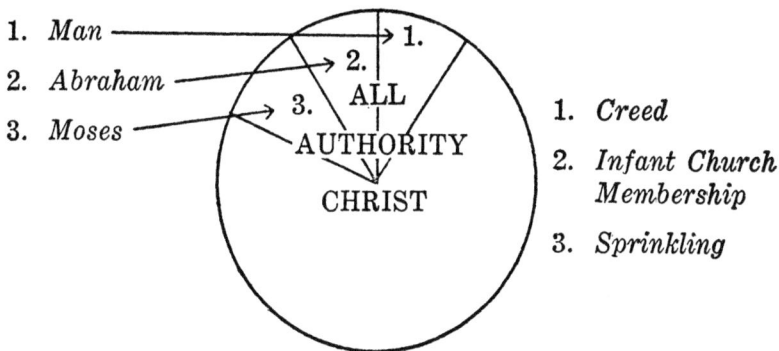

1. *Man*

2. *Abraham*

3. *Moses*

1.

2. ALL

3. AUTHORITY

CHRIST

1. *Creed*

2. *Infant Church Membership*

3. *Sprinkling*

What have we done now? We have taken another big slice out of the authority of the Lord Jesus Christ.

Now then I have one more. I know that the time is rapidly getting away, but I do want you to see it. This fourth one is the authority of Christ and the authority of man with regard to instrumental music in the worship. Now what is the authority for it? Well, it is not found in the New Testament. I just want to read you the passages rapidly that are found in the New Testament on the subject of the kind of music in the worship.

Matthew 26:30: "And when they had sung an hymn, they went out into the mount of Olives."

Mark 14:26 says the same thing.

Acts 16:25: "And at midnight Paul and Silas prayed, and sang praises unto God: and the prisoners heard them."

Romans 15:19: "For this cause I will confess to thee among the Gentiles, and sing unto thy name."

I Corinthians 14:15: "What is it then? I will pray with the spirit, and I will pray with the understanding also: I will sing with the spirit, and I will sing with the understanding also."

Ephesians 5:19: "Speaking to yourselves in psalms and hymns and spiritual songs, singing and making melody in your heart to the Lord."

Colossians 3:16: "Let the word of Christ dwell in you richly in all wisdom; teaching and admonishing one another in psalms and hymns and spiritual songs, singing with grace in your hearts to the Lord."

Hebrews 2:12: "Saying, I will declare thy name unto my brethren, in the midst of the church will I sing praise unto thee."

James 5:13: "Is any merry? let him sing psalms."

Now, friends, those are the nine passages of scripture in the New Testament that refer to the kind of music authorized in the New Testament worship. There is not one single solitary reference to instrumental music. I am not opposed to instrumental music. I am very fond of it for that matter. Out at Florida Christian College I get out with the boys sometimes and play in their little string band. We have a piano in our home, or we did have until my daughter married and carried it up to Floral City with her. Most Christians have instruments of various kinds in their homes. People say, "You folks just don't like music." Now that is not so. We do. We enjoy it very much, but not in the worship of the Lord. Why not? Because there is no authority for it. We move by the authority of the Lord, by the authority of Christ. We are not willing to chop up his authority like some people do, but we are simply going to do what the Lord says regarding worship.

But somebody says: "Oh, I remember that David said a great deal about music. I remember that David said, 'Praise him with the psaltry and harp.'" (Or a "peaseltree" as the old negro said when he read it.) David also said, "Praise him with the timbrel and dance." Psalms 150. By the same authority that you use David for instrumental music in the worship, then you can use him for the dance. Suppose we just clear this building out Saturday night (we are not going to have services Saturday night) and so we can just push these benches back and hire Vanny Sanders' orchestra and have a big dance. If anybody comes in and objects we will shout: "following David. David said, 'Praise him with the dance.'" Can you imagine Elwood Phillips and me in each other's arms (this will be scriptural dancing, not "mixed" dancing) swinging around until the wee small hours of the night, and shouting: "Praise the Lord; we got it from David." No, friends, that will never do. Look what you have done to the authority of the Lord Jesus Christ. You have David in the authority circle now.

1. *Man*
2. *Abraham*
3. *Moses*
4. *David*

1.
2.
3.
ALL
AUTHORITY
4.
CHRIST

1. *Creed*
2. *Infant Church Membership*
3. *Sprinkling*
4. *Instrumental Music in Worship*

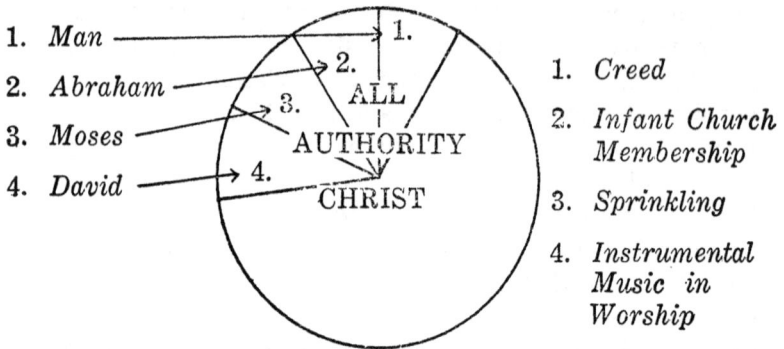

That just about winds it up it looks like to me. Look at it! You have men that make the creeds dividing the authority of the Lord. You have Abraham as authority for infant church membership. You can't get it from Christ, and so you go back to Abraham. You have Moses as the authority for sprinkling. You can't get it from Christ, so you go back to Moses. And you have David as authority for instrumental music because neither the Lord Jesus Christ or any of his apostles say a single word about it.

I am a most congenial fellow, at least I think so. I'm not cranky, at least I don't think I am. I don't want to be. I want to know and preach the truth and I want you to appreciate the fact that I have honestly presented to you tonight some of the teaching of God's divine will on *authority,* and knowing the difference between the authority of the Lord and the authority of men. Some day I shall leave this old earth, and I am going to stand before my God and give an account for this very sermon that I have preached to you tonight. When I stand before the Lord in the judgment he is going to judge me, not by what the counsels of men may say. He is not going to judge me by what Abraham has had to say. He is not going to judge me on the basis of what Moses has had to say with regard to my salvation as a member of the New Testament church. He is not going to judge me with what David said and what he commanded. The Bible says

He has committed ALL judgment UNTO HIS SON. He is the one you and I are going to stand before one of these days. Friends, have you been taking the word of some man about some of these things? You know, men are fallible, honest, but fallible. Don't you take Harry Pickup's word for authority; you search the Scriptures and see what God says about these matters and you understand what the Bible teaches, because one of these days you are going to stand before him and give an account for the way you have lived. You need to know the difference, and if you don't know the difference, it could mean the difference between your going to heaven and going to hell. Not because God doesn't want you to know the truth. God is not willing that any should perish, but is suffering long to usward, "not willing that any should perish, but that all should come to repentance." I didn't always understand this; I wasn't raised in the church of Christ. But one day I heard the gospel. It was a strange thing to me then; I didn't understand it. But I will tell you what convinced me, brother, I went to the old Book. I said, What does God want me to know about this, what is the authority? And I came to the conclusion that the authority is in Christ, not in man. Not in one man or a set of men, or a man that might have been a good man out of the Old Testament. The authority is in the Lord Jesus Christ. He is the one who is going to judge you some day, and it is my earnest, sincere prayer that you will take him for your guide. Let his word direct you in what you do. Try to know the difference. Don't throw this aside and say, "Well, that's just old Harry Pickup's idea." Please don't do that, because one day I have got to meet you in the judgment. You will be there and I'll be there. Every knee shall bow to Jesus and every tongue shall confess to God. You can't say, "Well, I followed what somebody told me was right." Yes, but Jesus is going to say to you in that day, "Depart from me ye that work iniquity, I never knew you."

"Why don't you know me, Lord?"

"Well, I will tell you why I don't. You are like the man that built his house on the sand; the rains descended, the floods came, the winds blew and beat upon that house and it fell and great was the fall of it."

Why? Because the foolish did not build upon the word of God. He didn't do the will of God, but he did the will of man. The man who built upon the solid rock of God's divine truth, is the man whose house, when the winds blew and the rains fell and the floods came and beat upon that house, fell not. Why? Because he was a wise man. How was he wise? He did the will of the Father. "Not everyone that saith unto me, Lord, Lord, shall enter into the kingdom of heaven, but he that doeth the will of my Father which is in heaven." I want you to think about it. If you follow the authority of the Lord and do Christ's will, all will be well.

Let me earnestly ask you tonight: believe in Christ with all your heart, turn away from error, from sin, turn from the things that are not in keeping with God's teaching, confess Christ before men, be buried in baptism for the remission of your sins. That, brother, is the teaching of Christ. That comes from HIS authority. Then rise to walk the new life, and walk it faithfully as long as God lets you live. "Be thou faithful unto death, and I will give thee a crown of life." That is the word of Christ. Do his will, trust him for his promises, and you will go to heaven when life is over. Will you come tonight while together we stand and sing?

HEAVEN AND WHO WILL GO THERE

Once again we want to express to you our personal appreciation for your presence, for the fact that you have come tonight to study with us God's divine will. We hope, as we think together about this message or this sermon, that you will ponder the truths presented in the light of your own case and render obedience unto God according to His will. We are discussing tonight a subject that is rather popular, one that all of us are interested in—some perhaps not as much so as we should be—and that is the subject of *Heaven and Who Will Go There.* As a background for what I want to say I am reading a portion of the first paragraph of the 14th chapter of the gospel of John. "Let not your heart be troubled: ye believe in God, believe also in me. In my Father's house are many mansions: if it were not so, I would have told you. I go to prepare a place for you. And if I go and prepare a place for you, I will come again, and receive you unto myself; that where I am, there ye may be also. And whither I go ye know, and the way ye know. Thomas saith unto him, Lord, we know not whither thou goest; and how can we know the way? Jesus saith unto him, I am the way, the truth, and the life: no man cometh unto the Father, but by me."

Those passages, my friends, introduce the idea that Christ has gone to prepare a place that the Bible refers to as heaven, and that it has been made ready for those who are making themselves ready for it. We want to consider tonight some of the lessons God teaches on the subject of *Heaven and Who Will Go There.*

I am conscious of the fact that there is almost always a positive and a negative side to every sermon topic or study. Now I believe that is true with the subject that I have announced for tonight. I mean that the negative side will often bring out what is the real proof respecting the delusions of men regarding whether they are going or not. In the words of the old song that the negroes sing, and I have heard the Fisk Jubilee Singers sing the song many times, "Everybody talking about heaven ain't a going there." I believe that is so. The reason I believe that is so is because of the significance attached to passages of scripture in the Bible about that subject. Sometimes though, people will say, "I am sure this individual has gone to heaven. He was my relative and he was a very good man, a good grandfather or a good grandmother, or some other good relative of mine that I know has gone to heaven because that person was so good." Well, do you know, friends, there is something strange about that. While, of course, God expects man to be good and honorable and just in his dealings with his fellowman (and that is what people usually mean when they make that statement) there is not such a statement in all the Bible which predicates salvation on man's being good. In answer to the question, "What Must I Do To Be Saved?" "He that is a good man and is kind to his fellowman shall be saved" is not in the Bible. Now obviously God expects men to be good and honorable and conscientious, about their dealings with their fellowman, and we have examples of good honorable people. The man, Cornelius, by the way, was a very conscientious, sincere individual. The point of the matter is, my friends, that going to heaven is not based upon moral goodness alone, but there are other things that God expects men to do in order to be prepared for that place about which the Lord Jesus Christ said, "I go to prepare a place for you: and if I go and prepare a place for you, I will come again, and receive you unto myself; that where I am, there ye may be also."

I recognize the fact that Jesus was talking to his disciples. He said I am going away and I'm going to come back, and my job while I'm gone is to prepare a place for you, among other things. Our Lord made that statement. Now who is going with him? Who will be with the Lord in that place that Christ refers to as the prepared place which he has made ready for those who do his will?

I want to consider some negative points tonight that I think should be considered because there is so much in

the world today that is misleading. Take the statement
I made a moment ago. Why without any consideration for
what is the truth of the matter, we just dismiss it and say,
"I suppose that is all right." I remember some few years
ago I preached the funeral of a man, or rather I assisted
in it—I tried to get out of it—who was an aged individual,
and he had been an infidel all his life so far as I knew. I
met him late in life, through some of his children who were
members of the body of Christ. I had visited the old man
and talked to him some about the Bible. He didn't believe
in Jesus Christ as the Son of God, and he apparently didn't
believe the Bible was the word of God, if what he told me
was the true state of his mind on the matter. It was not
long after I met him until he died. They didn't ask me to
preach the funeral, the family didn't, but I was there and
the preacher who did preach the funeral, knowing that I was
the preacher at the congregation where some of the members of the family attended services, he just insisted that
I have a part in the funeral. Well, I couldn't do anything
else but go ahead, and so I sat on the stand and listened to
what he had to say about the old fellow. He talked about
his good points, and that is very nice and kind and consid-
erate and I'm sure nothing wrong is done by talking about
the good in people. You know, it was once said that the
"evil that men do lives after them, but the good is oft in-
terred with their bones." That is true. We doubtless don't
say enough good about people. But that preacher went
on further than that. He said, "Now I know this man
wasn't a Christian, but he has gone to heaven; he is there
in heaven." Now I knew if the old man expressed his faith
to me correctly, he didn't believe in the Bible as the word
of God. How can a man go to heaven that doesn't have
any faith in the Lord who has gone to prepare the place?
Well, you perhaps have a pretty good idea of what I had to
say about that. I just couldn't allow those people to leave
with that idea in mind. I didn't get into it; somebody
pushed me into it. (I never do get into those things, you
know, they just look me up and you have to do something

kindly that some things said were not true.)   Well, the
preacher got awfully mad at me.   All I did was read a few
passages of scripture and make a brief comment.   There
would have been many people who would have gone away
from the cemetery in ignorance.   I had to make my little
speech after the man's body had been put away in the
ground, and while the crowd was still there, not to inter-
rupt his service, but I had to do it.   The preacher became
quite angry.   Some people believe that because a man is
good, that death brings dignity to his actions, but that isn't
true.   To some it doesn't make any difference how a man
has lived, when he dies, they think he goes to heaven anyway.   That is not so; hence we need to do some negative
thinking about such matters and that is my reason for all
I have said in the foregoing in order to say this that I am
going to say now.

I am reading a passage of scripture from the 7th chapter of the book of Matthew and verse 21: "Not every one
that saith unto me, Lord, Lord, shall enter into the kingdom of heaven: but he that doeth the will of my Father
which is in heaven.   Many will say to me in that day, Lord,
Lord, have we not prophesied in thy name?   and in thy
name have cast out devils?   and in thy name done many
wonderful works?   And then will I profess unto them, I
never knew you: depart from me, ye that work iniquity."

Now, friends, you need to think about that and so do I.
Heaven, and who is going there!   Well I will tell you, the
fellow who has not obeyed God isn't going there.   That is
what Jesus is talking about in that passage of scripture.
You may think that you are going to heaven, and I may
think that I am going to heaven, but that passage of scripture teaches (if the Lord knew what he was talking about
and I certainly know that he did) that "not every one who
says, Lord, Lord," is going to heaven.   He said many people
are going to say, "Lord, Lord," but I am going to say back
to them, "I never knew you."

"Lord, you don't know me?"

"No, sir, I don't know you."

"Well, why not?"

"I don't know you because you didn't do the will of my Father which is in heaven."

Now that is the point. It is not how people feel; it is not what they think; it is not what you believe about the matter; but it is actually what you have proved you believe, by what you have done. The Bible teaches that God would send a strong delusion, a working of error, that they all may believe a lie, that they all may be damned who believed not the truth, but had pleasure in unrighteousness. Now listen: It is not believing that saves a man, it is WHAT he believes. You have got to believe the truth. You may believe error and be damned. That fellow did who came to the Lord in the last day. He was a religious man, he was a consecrated and conscientious individual, but he hadn't done the Lord's will.

I want to write on the blackboard tonight a few of these negative things that people believe in but that are wrong, and the first one is:

1. AN ALIEN SINNER.

Now why was he an alien sinner? Reasoning from Matthew 7:21, the man said, "Don't you know me?"

"No!"

Now what is the significance of the statement: "I know you not"? He had not done the will of his Father, had not done the will of God, and therefore, because he had not done the will of God he was not in the right kingdom; he was not in the right relationship unto the Lord. That is the reason. It doesn't mean by that expression that the Lord didn't know the man's name; that the Lord didn't know who he was talking to; that the Lord didn't know that this person lived on the earth and that he has now come up before him in the judgment. That is a judgment scene. You know, Jesus talked about a lot of things in the sermon on the mount. He told them the difference be-

tween the law of Moses and the law of Christ; he showed
them the importance of the law of Christ over the law of
Moses, that it was greater than the law of Moses. He
talked about dealing with your fellowman, and finally he
pointed out what it is going to be like in the judgment.
People are going to cry out unto him. They are going to
say, "Lord, Lord," but he is going to say, "I don't know
you." What is wrong? "You haven't done the will of my
Father who is in heaven."

You know, sometimes people say, "That is the trouble
with you people. You don't believe there is but one church."
Who said anything about not believing there is but one
church? Why I believe there are lots of churches. There
is the Methodist Church, the Baptist Church, the Presbyterian Church, the Catholic Church, the Episcopalian
Church and many others. There are several hundred in
this country of ours, different distinct denominations, all
of them teaching, at least to some extent, radically different ideas, some of them with doctrines that are diametri-
cally opposed to the position of other churches on how to
go to heaven. No, it isn't a question of not believing there
is but one church. There are lots of churches in the world,
my friends. The word *Church* is not an uncommon word
especially. It simply means a body of individuals that are
called out of another group for some specific purpose, just
to be brief about it. Now my point is not about whether
or not that are many churches; my point is, can you go to
heaven in them? I want you to see that. There are lots
of churches, but does the Lord have one and what did he
mean when he made the statement, "I don't know you"?
Why he is simply saying, "Brother, you are in the wrong
one." Now let me read another passage for you. In Acts
2:47, after Peter had preached that first sermon on the
day of Pentecost, in which men and women cried out and
said: "Men and brethren, what shall we do?" he told them
what to do, and verse 47 says, "And the Lord added to the
church daily such as should be saved." Now you watch
this reasoning for just a moment. Who does the adding

to the church? The Bible says the Lord does. You can
go join some denomination if you want to. That is your
privilege, that is your right, and far be it from me to say
that you don't have that right. You can join anything
you want to. You can identify yourself with any religious
movement that you choose. And I am glad that we are
not hindered by some government that will not permit us
to study the Bible and serve God according to the teaching
of the Bible. Brother Dumm prayed in the prayer tonight
and thanked God for the fact that we can come into this
building and serve the Lord and preach his gospel without
the authorities closing the doors. Any religious body has
that same right, and while I wouldn't believe what the
fellow teaches, I will defend his right to teach it because
I believe he has a right according to the government to
teach anything that he desires. That is not the point.
The point is: can he go to heaven and believe something
the Bible doesn't authorize?

The Bible says that the Lord adds people to the church.
That is not hard to understand. Well, what church does
He add them to? Let me read another passage for you
and I'll tell you. In the 16th chapter of the book of Matthew and verse 18, Jesus came into the coasts of Caesarea
Philippi, he came to his disciples and said, Whom do men
say that I the Son of man am? And they said, Some say
that you are John the Baptist, some Elias and some Jeremias or one of the prophets. And he said to them, Whom
say ye that I am? And now verse 16: "And Simon Peter
answered and said, Thou are the Christ, the Son of the
living God. And Jesus answered and said unto him, Blessed
art thou, Simon Barjona: for flesh and blood hath not revealed it unto thee, but my Father which is in heaven.
And I say also unto thee, That thou art Peter," now watch,
"and upon this rock I will build MY CHURCH; and the
gates of hell shall not prevail against it." Who is talking?
Christ is the one that is talking, and he said, "MY
CHURCH." All right, that is the church of Christ. You
couldn't miss that to save your soul. I don't care what

the preacher has said to you about it, you couldn't miss
that. What did the Lord say? He said, "Upon this rock
I will build MY CHURCH." That is what I mean when I
talk about the church of Christ. That is what I mean;
that is what the Bible teaches.

Now look: If the Lord said, "I have a church," and if
the Lord does the adding to the church, which church does
he add them to? What would you say? If you didn't
know a thing in the world about the Bible, if you didn't
know one thing in the world about religion, you couldn't
miss that. If the Lord has a church, (and Matthew 16:
18, 19 says he has) and if the Lord does the adding, (and
Acts 2:47 says he does) what church does he add them
to? Do you suppose he adds them to various and sundry
sectarian organizations that are not the one which he established? That is the thing I want you to see.

What was wrong with those men in Matthew 7:21-27?
They were in the wrong kingdom, identified with the wrong
group. Were they sincere? I have no right on earth to
question their motives and desires. Well, if one was honestly mistaken can't he still go to heaven? Why, friends,
you don't even obey the laws of the land that way. You
drive your car down Ft. Harrison Avenue here in front of
this church building at 50 miles an hour and go through
every red light, the chances are if you don't run over somebody or have an accident an officer will probably stop you,
or somebody else will, and they will say, "Let's go down
and talk to the judge about this." When you get down
there you say, "Oh, judge, I didn't know it was wrong to
run a red light; I didn't know it was wrong to run 50 miles
an hour down Ft. Harrison Avenue." Now you just wouldn't
do that. You would not plead the fact that you were honest
in your violation, and the judge would not pay any attention to it if you did.

I knew of a young man that spent 20 years in the state
pen just near Nashville, Tennessee, whose plea was, "I
didn't know it was wrong to kill a man." I will not tell you
the details about it, but that young man was honest about

it. He was raised up in the mountains where some people do not seem to know whether or not there are any laws that regulate men in matters of that kind. They move according to their own laws in some of those communities. I have held meetings in some of those places and I know whereof I speak. It is not a laughing matter. It is something that is serious. This boy came from that community and he told the judge: "I didn't know it was wrong to kill some dog that got in my way," meaning the fellow he killed. The judge said, "Well, you will find out. We are going to give you 20 years to think it over." Friends, people don't act that way with regard to anything except religion—I mean intelligent people.

There was an old friend of mine—now passed and gone—whose name was G. W. Sweeney, and he used to make this statement: "Folks will act reasonably sensible about anything in the world except religion and politics." I think that is right. We will take the craziest positions, in spite of what the Bible says about it, on many things in religion, and we would not do that for anything in other matters. Now then, alien sinners—people who haven't obeyed God, who haven't obeyed the gospel—will not be in the heavenly home. Heaven and who is going there! Negatively speaking, not those who have disobeyed God.

But I want you to notice one other point with regard to this. Back in the Old Testament we read the story of Noah and the ark. I believe that record just as God teaches it in His word. I think Noah did build an ark according to the teaching of the Bible, and according to the instructions laid down by God for him to build it. Finally, the heavens opened and the floods came and everybody that was in the ark was saved, with all the animals that Noah had gotten in there. There is a lot of misunderstanding regarding the ark, but I believe exactly what the Book says. Some folks say that God just couldn't make an ark big enough for that, and I won't have time to go into that tonight, although I would be glad to. Fact of the matter is the Bible says that those inside the ark were saved, and that is what I am interested in just here. Peter comments on it in I Peter 3:20, 21. He said there wasn't anybody saved but Noah and his family. Well, there were a lot of good old grandmas and grandpas around there then, and I have an idea that they did everything in their power, after they saw that the proverbial "jig" was up, so to speak, to get out of that water. I have an idea that they may have improvised structures of some kind to keep from drowning for a while, but everyone that was not in that ark was lost. Do you believe that? You have got to if you believe the Bible, because the Bible says there were only eight souls saved, and the authority for it is I Peter 3:20. You can go back and read the record in the book of Genesis where it says the same thing. Now then, who is going to heaven? Those who do God's will. Those who do not God's will—that is the alien sinner—are not going to heaven because they are in the wrong place, with the wrong people, in the wrong kingdom.

Well, let us notice another group and talk about them a little while. The scripture is Matthew 23, beginning with verse 13 and reading through verse 15. Jesus is talking to a group of people and he said: "Woe unto you, scribes and Pharisees, hypocrites! for ye shut up the kingdom of heaven against men: for ye neither go in yourselves, neither suffer ye them that are entering to go in. Woe unto you, scribes and Pharisees, hypocrites! for ye devour widows' houses, and for a pretence make long prayer: therefore ye shall receive the greater damnation. Woe unto you, scribes and Pharisees, hypocrites! for ye compass sea and land to make one proselyte, and when he is made, ye make him twofold more the child of hell than yourselves." Now look at this: (writes on the blackboard).

2. HYPOCRITES.

Jesus stated on that occasion that those who are hypocritical, those who devour widow's houses, (a figure of speech) had better look out. They are pretending to be something but slyly they are taking away the living of these poor unfortunate widows. Because they are doing that Jesus says they are going to receive a greater condemnation. These were the religious leaders of that day, by the way. They were hypocritical in their attitude about life; they were the leaders of Judaism, but they were "playing the game," they were but pretending. That word comes from the Greek word "hupokritas." It is the word that means in the Greek "to play on the stage; a stage player; a pretender; one who plays on the stage." What were these people doing? They were wearing a long face, and I can imagine they went about with their hands behind them, and as they intoned their messages to the people with a pretended piety, by which some of the people, who didn't know any better, were completely deceived. But the Lord Jesus Christ looked into their hearts and he said: "You hypocrites, you are going to be lost; your condemnation is going to be greater than anybody else." Now why? "You are playing on the stage." Friends, hypocrites are not going to be saved in heaven according to the statement made by the Lord on that occasion. Why not? They have the wrong kind of heart, that is why. What kind of a heart have they got? They have a hypocritical heart, and that is the reason they are not going to heaven. They play both ends against the middle, so to speak. They are playing at the subject of Christianity, if we apply that to the church of God today and that is what I am doing.

I have heard people say, "I just don't like hypocrites because they are just playing at it and that is one of the reasons why I don't obey the gospel, because there are so many hypocrites in the church." Well, you know it is unfortunate, but there are hypocrites everywhere and once in a while one of them does get in the church; in fact there might be several. But there are not any more in the church, in fact there are not as many, as out of the church. Suppose you were planning to join a business organization as an employee, say one of the big department stores, and you were offered a lucrative salary, and the work was appealing to you—the very kind you would like to do. You went down and looked the matter over; the boss thought you were going to accept the job, and you were about to, but when you get ready to sign the application blank and start to work, you say: "Oh, no, you have too many hypocrites in this organization." Friends, you know you wouldn't do that. If that were so, nobody would ever get married because some people could surely say, "I know a woman who married a hypocrite. (I know none of the old maids would say that.) I am sure that there are few people that would proceed on such a basis because there are some hypocrites in the world, and a few women will marry them. Some men are simply playing at the game of being good husbands, but people go right on getting married in spite of the fact that they know about it. And here is something else that I want to say along that line: you need not worry about that hypocrite. If there IS a hypocrite in the church, you need not worry about him because the Bible teaches that he is not going to be saved. And I'll tell you something else: Don't play the buzzard with regard to Christianity. You know how the buzzard does; you have seen them flying around here in Florida, and the only thing they are looking for is the carcass of some dead animal that they can pick on. Well, the hypocrite is already dead, so don't you play the part of a buzzard with regard to him and pick on him and let that keep you from becoming a Christian.

I used to know a member of the church who said, "I just can't go to church because every time I go I see this individual who is such a rotten hypocrite, and sometimes they will even ask him to pass the Lord's Supper and I just can't stand it." You don't have to be uneasy about that, my brother, my sister. If there happens to be some, and I have an idea that you will find some almost everywhere who are playing at the game of being a Christian, you need not be uneasy, you will not have to spend any time with them if you go to heaven, because they will not be there. But if you don't go to heaven, you will have to spend eternity with them in hell, because that is where they are going to be.

Now there is another one that I want you to notice, and this will be the last one for this evening because it takes a little longer than the others. It is based on a passage in Revelation 3:15,16. Jesus is speaking to John as John is writing this. He says: "I know thy works, that thou art neither cold nor hot: I would thou wert cold or hot. So then because thou art lukewarm, and neither cold nor hot, I will spue thee out of my mouth." Now what do we have there? It is not the alien sinner, and it is not the hypocrite. Well, who is it? He is the (writes on blackboard)

3. LUKEWARM CHRISTIAN.

A member of the church? Yes, sir. What is wrong with him? Let us see. Hear the passage in verse 17: "Because thou sayest, I am rich and increased with goods, and have need of nothing; and knowest not that thou art wretched, and miserable, and poor, and blind, and naked." That is what is wrong with that fellow. I used to think that a lukewarm Christian was an individual who was sort of indifferent, but that is not the meaning of that word altogether. We say that a man isn't cold nor hot, but do we know what we mean by "he is not cold nor hot"? How long since you have got right down to the bed rock principles of Christianity in serving the Lord by visiting the sick, or calling on someone that needed your help, or doing anything of the many things that people do in serving God and doing His will as Chritsians? God commands us to "visit the fatherless and widows in their afflictions" as well as "keep yourself unspotted from the world." Sometimes members of the church will become lukewarm in that respect, but that is not the whole meaning of it. Let me show you something else. The Bible says that you need to recognize that you need eye-salve "to anoint thine eyes that thou mayest see." Now watch! This lukewarm Christian needs knowledge. Knowledge of what? Knowledge of

God's divine word. They had lost their knowledge of God's divine word. That was one of the characteristics of lukewarmness in the church. Not just the fact that he doesn't come to services, not just the fact that he doesn't visit the sick, not just the fact that he is not concerned about the work of the Lord. That is all included, but the Bible says that this fellow who is lukewarm, and is to be spued out of the mouth of God at the last day, is not going to be in heaven. What is wrong with him? First, he needs knowledge. He is lacking in knowledge of God's divine will.

God expects you Christians to grow. In II Peter 1:5 to 7 we read: "And besides this, giving all diligence, add to your faith virtue; and to virtue knowledge; and to knowledge temperance; and to temperance patience; and to patience godliness; and to godliness brotherly kindness; and to brotherly kindness charity." And then Peter said in the last thing that he ever wrote: "But grow in grace, and in the knowledge of our Lord and Saviour Jesus Christ." You have the responsibility of adding the Christian virtues. You have the responsibility of growing in grace and knowledge of Jesus Christ. If you are one of those members of the church who only comes on rare occasions, perhaps just during a meeting, occasionally just drop in on Sunday morning, you need to do something about your condition because the chances are that you are lacking in knowledge. One of the characteristics of that individual who is lukewarm is the lack of knowledge.

Let me read another one. Not only has he failed with regard to his need for knowledge but according to this statement, "Buy of me gold tried in the fire," that individual has lost his sense of true value. "Buy of me gold." What is gold? Gold is the standard of judgment with respect to purity, and this individual has lost his sense of true values with regard to spiritual matters. Friends, I sometimes liken it unto this: I have always been interested in music, but I have never moved in that higher sphere up here where actually in my heart I long to move. I can listen to a rich symphony over the radio and can only appreciate certain parts of it because my musical education is so limited. I can listen to a concerto or I can listen to some beautiful song of the classical type sung by a talented individual, and, although I am grasping up here, I am sort of down here in the Hill-Billy category. You can play "I'm Coming Around The Mountain" and I know what you are talking about. You can play others of the Hill-Billy songs, and I understand them, yet there is a desire in my heart to learn and appreciate classical music. I will tell you, friends, I think there are members of the church today who have lost their true sense of value and who are, spiritually speaking, unable to appreciate the true value of Christianity. I think that is so. We need to buy some gold tried in fire because we have lost our true sense of value from a spiritual viewpoint.

Let me give you another example. Here is an individual who once knew the truth and appreciated it, but he has wandered away and has lost his knowledge to such an extent that he has, for all practical purposes, left the church. Maybe he has gone out yonder and joined himself to something that the Bible says nothing about, and then he begins to "hem and haw"—apologize for error and sectarianism and division. What has he done? He has lost his true sense of value; he has lost his knowledge of God's divine will. He wouldn't be classed as a lukewarm Christian by us, perhaps. What is wrong with him? He has lost his sense of appreciation of the finer spiritual values that are found in the Christian life. When he begins to think in terms of humanism, and human affairs and material things, and lets them monopolize him and control his whole thinking, then there is not very much that you can do with him. He apologizes for error; he apologizes for the filthy, trashy things that people see in the moving picture shows, on the stage, or read in the magazines, and his appreciation of things has sunk to a very low level. What is the matter? He used to be a faithful Christian, but he has generated to the point where he needs to buy gold tried in fire; he needs to get his sense of spiritual values back where it was with God.

But that is not all. Listen to this: "And white raiment, that thou mayest be clothed, and that the shame of thy nakedness do not appear." He needs to recognize the fact that he has disregarded, or has failed to regard, mercy and righteousness. Mercy, righteousness, honorable thinking, honorable conduct, we don't often think of them as characteristics of a lukewarm Christian, do we? We think of the lukewarm Christian as negligent, neither in nor out, perhaps not enjoying anything especially; we think of him as one who is perfectly genial about the church, but he just doesn't come like he should. We measure it in terms of whether he comes to church or not as to whether he is lukewarm or not. That is not the Biblical meaning of the word "lukewarm" altogether. I believe I could say in just a few words that there are a few pitiable souls in the church today who only have enough Christianity to make them miserable; not enough to really enjoy the fellowship of the saints of God and the beauty of holiness and the happiness and joy of doing God's will. They are miserable because they have just enough religion that when you talk to them about knowledge they squirm and twist and say, "I don't get any pleasure out of the study of the Bible. It is so dry that I don't enjoy it." Those people have no true sense of value of what is right or good, and have failed to regard mercy and righteousness as the Bible regards them: white raiments that they may clothe themselves. Friends, what is wrong with those individuals? What is the matter with the persons described here? I'll tell you. They are emphasizing the wrong things in this life. I conclude, that as the alien sinner is in the wrong kingdom, the hypocrite has the wrong kind of heart, the lukewarm Christian is emphasizing the wrong thing. He will not go to heaven.

But now let us notice a very important positive idea: Who is going to heaven? I want to close the sermon at the place where I began just a while ago: Matthew 7:21. "Not everyone that saith unto me, Lord, Lord, shall enter into the kingdom of heaven; but he that doeth the will of my Father which is in heaven." Can you see that Bible from where you are? (Puts open Bible on stand before audience.) Can you see that Bible? I often say I wish I had a book big enough so that it would cover the whole end of the building so that as you sit in your seat where you are and as I turn the pages, you could sit anywhere in the building and read the letters on it: read the verses on it. You can't see the wording from where you are sitting unless you have mighty good eyes. Now listen: The Bible says the fellow is going to heaven who does the will of God, and this is the will of God concerning you. (Points to the Bible.) It tells you what to do to be a Christian, what church to be a member of, how to worship scripturally, and how to live the Christian life so you can go to heaven when life is over. That Book tells it, brother, you don't need to depend on someone who may be concerned about his own ideas, you don't have to ask some preacher what to do to be saved. Some people say, "Well, my preacher says this, my preacher says that." When people learn that preachers say a lot of things besides their prayers, there will be a lot more names inscribed on the Lamb's Book of Life. I want you to remember that. Don't you trust any man with regard to that which concerns your soul. You read it from God's divine will.

I want to read a passage from the last book in the Bible, the 20th chapter of the book of Revelation: "And I saw the dead, small and great, stand before God; and the books were opened: and another book was opened, which is the book of life: and the dead were judged out of those things which were written in the books, according to their works." That is the thing you are going to be judged by. God's new covenant, the New Testament, which came into effect with the death of the Lord. It is the new covenant, the New Testament. You are NOT going to be judged by human creeds or what the preachers say. You are going to be judged by what that Book says. Those are the ones who are going to heaven; those who are responding to the instructions found in that Book. What does that Book say? The Book says that you must be a Christian. Let me read it for you. Acts 11:26: "And the disciples were called CHRISTIANS first at Antioch." And Peter commenting on the name said: "Neither is there salvation in any other name: for there is none other name under heaven given among men, whereby we must be saved." If you have something else in addition to the name *Christian* you have got too much. What are you going to do with that when you stand before God in the judgment? You are a member of some organization that has given you another name, what are you going to say about that in the judgment? The Book says you must believe in the Lord with all your heart. "Faith cometh by hearing, and hearing by the word of God." "Without faith it is impossible to please him: for he that cometh to God must believe that he is, and that he is a rewarder of them that diligently seek him." Now if you don't believe in Christ, brother, what are you going to do at the last day? You say, "Oh, I thought he was just a man." You just thought wrong; the Bible says he is the Son of God, and your salvation depends upon it. When you come before him at the great day and say, "Lord, I was an agnostic, I just didn't know, and so I just never did do anything about you." The Lord will say: "Depart from me ye that work iniquity, I never knew you." The Bible says that you must believe in the Lord with all your heart. You have got to be a Christian. The Bible says that you must repent of your sins. "The time of this ignorance God winked at;" that was back in the old times, God overlooked their sins and weaknesses, not that He did not demand that they obey Him, but He was merciful to them in view of them being under a school master looking to the time when the complete revelation would be theirs, "but now commandeth all men everywhere to repent." God expects you to repent of your sins. He required that under the old law too, but there were different circumstances involved than under the new. So what are you going to say if you come to the Lord in the judgment and haven't repented of your sins? Jesus said: "Whosoever therefore shall confess me before men, him will I confess also before my Father which is in heaven." That means you. Then you need to be buried in baptism for the remission of your sins. "Oh, but I don't think I want to be buried; I don't want to get all wet." Now you just listen to this passage— Romans 6:4: "Therefore we are buried with him by baptism into death: that like as Christ was raised up from the dead by the glory of the Father, even so we also should walk in newness of life." The Lord was buried in the tomb, completely buried out of sight. You must be buried in the act of baptism, and as you are buried in baptism it is for the remission of your sins. People say, "Well, I just can't see that." The trouble is that you are looking at something else and not looking at what God said about it.

Now, friends, that is the teaching of the Bible about WHO will be saved: those who DO the will of God, those who LIVE the will of God; those children of God who WOR-SHIP according to the will of God. To them Jesus is going to say, "Come, ye blessed of my Father, inherit the king-dom prepared for you from the foundation of the world."

Are you here tonight not a member of the church that you can read about in that Book that is open before you? It is going to be open before you in the judgment, brother, so you had better see what it contains. You had better not trust what the preacher says about it, or what somebody else has said about it that mislead you. You can read for yourself. Can you read the name you wear, religiously speaking, in that Book? Can you read from it what you did in becoming what you are? Can you read about the things you do in worship from that Book, or do you have to get another one to tell you how to worship? I think you can see this. I hope you do. I want you to go to heaven, and I assure you I want to go to heaven. I don't want to be lost. I spend much time trying to lead people to Christ, sometimes making people offended because I just can't go along with them, but determined to go along with this Book. I had much rather agree with folk. I am an agreeable individual really. I love people and I want people to love me, but when it comes to this, I have got to follow the teaching of God. Will you come tonight, obey His gospel. There is a great day coming and when that day comes you are going to stand before Christ in the judgment. As we sing about it I hope that you will come forward tonight and give Brother Phillips your hand.

THE JUDGMENT DAY

Once again, friends, I am happy to stand before you, not only before you but before the Lord, and reason with you about some of the things that God would have us to know about His will, and try if possible to present the gospel in such a way that men and women can understand it, and understanding it, will have the disposition to accept it. My business here is to preach the truth, present the word of God, lead men to Christ, and help to build up the cause of Christ by learning His will and following the teaching that God has revealed.

We have had a number of questions during the meeting. I have a couple of questions tonight that I want to talk about for a little while. The first one is stated like this: "How is one to do something about his salvation when he is dead in sin?" This came about as a result of the sermon last Friday evening. Somebody objected to the fact that it is possible for one to come. How is he going to do anything about it when he is dead in sin? Well, I would like to read several passages, and I think we can clear that up in a few moments. First of all I want you to notice some statements found in Ephesians 2:1: "And you hath he quickened, who were dead in trespasses and sins; wherein in time past ye walked according to the course of this world." There is a group of people who were once dead in sin. They were the Ephesian brethren, those people in the church in Ephesus. Paul goes on to discuss their condition, how they followed the prince of the power of the air, and then in verse 4: "But God, who is rich in mercy, for his great love wherewith he loved us, even when we were dead in sins, hath quickened us together with Christ, (by grace ye are saved;) and hath raised us up together, and made us sit together in heavenly places in Christ Jesus." The 7th verse refers to the fact that in the ages to come he might show the exceeding riches of his grace in kindness toward us in Christ. Now the Bible says that the way in which a person is made

97

alive from his sins is to get into Christ. That is the way
it is done. Man is unable to make a plan of his own that
will raise him up when he is dead in trespasses and sins;
he can't formulate a plan of his own to do it. Well, what
does he do? He simply lays hold on the plan of God, he
accepts the way of the Lord. What will that do for him?
That will put him in Christ. Now I want you to notice
a statement in Romans to continue for a few moments
with that idea. How does a man get into Christ? Now
you listen. In Romans 6:3 Paul says, and he is talking
not only to those people there, but to you and me today,
"What shall we say then? Shall we continue in sin, that
grace may abound? God forbid." How are we going to
do something about this? "How shall we, that are dead
to sin, live any longer therein? Know ye not, that so
many of us as were baptized into Jesus Christ were baptized into his death? That is the way you get into Christ,
friends. Now note the reason. Number one, here is a
man dead in sin; he can't do anything about his condition,
is the assumption. That is right, he can't do anything
about his condition so far as his making a plan to save
himself is concerned. He can't do that. We are his work-
manship, created in Christ Jesus unto good works, which
God hath before ordained that we should walk in them.
Walk in what? Walk in the works that God made. There
is no difference between the way Paul puts it in Ephesians
and the way he puts it here in his letter to the church at
Rome. Now notice one other thought. "Therefore we are
buried with him by baptism into death: that like as Christ
was raised up from the dead by the glory of the Father,
even so we also should walk in newness of life." There
are people who were once dead in sin, just like the Ephesians were dead in sin. To the church at Ephesus he told
them that the thing they must do in order to become alive
was to get into Christ. That is what gives the power;
that is what gives the life. There is no life, spiritually
speaking, for one dead in sin outside of Christ. What
does he do? He gets into Christ. How does he do it?

Well, he has to accept the Lord; he has to believe on him; he has to understand his will and then be baptized into Christ.

But I want to read another one. This one is from the second chapter of Acts, and I think it is very clear. Here in about the middle of the chapter—in verse 22—Peter is discussing with them the fact of the death and resurrection of Christ. He says: "Ye men of Israel, hear these words; Jesus of Nazareth, a man approved of God among you by miracles and wonders and signs, which God did by him in the midst of you, as ye yourselves also know: him, being delivered by the determinate counsel and foreknowledge of God, ye have taken, and by wicked hands have crucified and slain." These men had crucified the Lord. Were they dead in sin? I don't see how a man can be more dead in sin than they were. I don't see how he could get any further away from God than to crucify the Lord. That is about the top crime so far as the Bible is concerned. As he goes on, Peter charges them again with the same crime in verse 36. He says: "Therefore let all the house of Israel know assuredly, that God hath made that same Jesus, whom ye have crucified, both Lord and Christ." There is no doubt about their condition. When they heard that they were pricked in their hearts and said unto Peter and the rest of the apostles: "Men and brethren, what shall we do? Then Peter said unto them, Repent, and be baptized every one of you in the name of Jesus Christ for the remission of sins, and ye shall receive the gift of the Holy Ghost. For the promise is unto you, and to your children, and to all that are afar off, even as many as the Lord our God shall call." Now watch: "And with many other words did he testify and exhort, saying, Save yourself from this untoward generation." What are they going to do? There is only one thing that they can do and that is to save themselves by obeying Peter's instructions. The Bible says in verse 41: "Then they that gladly received his word were baptized: and the same day there were added unto them about three thousand souls." I'll tell you how that lines up, my friends. First, these people were dead in sin. How do I know they were? They had crucified the Lord. I know it because they couldn't do anything worse than that. If the Ephesians were dead in sin, and if the Romans were dead in sin, then the people on the day of Pentecost were dead in sin, because they did something infinitely worse when they crucified the Lord Jesus Christ. Peter said to them, when they cried out and said we don't know what to do— "Men and brethren, what shall we do?"—the thing you must do is to repent of your sins. What are those sins? One of them is the crucifixion of Jesus Christ, the Son of God. Then they "gladly received the word" after Peter said, "Save yourselves from this untoward generation." But denominational preachers tell us today that you can't save yourself. Well, that is what Peter told them on the day of Pentecost. If you know what he is talking about you can understand why he said it, and you can say the same thing today.

When I say to you, "Save yourselves from this wicked generation," that doesn't mean for you to go out and make a plan of your own; you just accept the plan that God has made for saving your soul. That is all you can do, scripturally. All those who received his word did that, and the Bible says the Lord added them to the church, Acts 2:47. Now what do we have here? Some preachers try to leave the impression that all you have to do is wait until the Holy Spirit comes down and does something to you. The thing that is wrong with that is that the Bible doesn't say a word about it. There is not an example in the entire Bible where God ever told anybody to wait for the Spirit, and while he is waiting to say the name of Jesus over and over as fast as he can, and finally he will get religion or something. That is just not in the Bible. The Bible says the way people are saved from their trespasses and sins—people who are dead in trespasses and sin—is to accept the plan of God. If they do not they are going to be dead in trespasses and sin when Jesus comes.

Here is question number two: The Bible says—and this is from the same person—we are saved by the blood, how about that? Well, I will tell you about that. In Acts 20:28 Paul said that Jesus purchased the church with his own blood, therefore, we are saved by his blood. If he saves the church with his blood, and we are in the church, then he saves us with his blood. We are bought by the blood of Christ; we are redeemed by the blood of the Lord. But look here: not only are we purchased, or bought, or redeemed or saved by the blood, but in Ephesians 2:8 Paul says we are saved by faith. Now then, are you going to accept both of them? Why sure. We can go still further and read the 9th verse and say we are saved by grace. Do you believe that too? Why sure. Now if I say you are saved by grace, what are you going to do about the passage that says you are saved by faith? Well, I will accept that too. I believe that you are saved by faith. Now you just watch again: In I Peter 3:21 Peter said we are saved by baptism. What would you do with that? Well, I will do the same thing with that I do with the others: I believe them both and practice them both. I could go on still further. In Acts 4:12 we see that we are saved by the name. I believe that just like I do the others. And in Romans 8:24 we are saved by hope. Now, brother, I believe all of them, and I can give you several more things by which we are saved. But here is the point: I do not believe that any one of these things is more important than any other one of them, but some people do. You may hear a man on the radio and he says all you have to do is to get down by your radio, believe in the Lord and give yourself up to Jesus and you are saved—saved by faith.

Friends, I believe you are saved by faith. No one preacher has a monopoly on information or understanding of God's divine word, or upon piety or faith. I can have just as much. The only thing, my friends, is that when somebody comes along and puts the word ONLY before any one of those words, that is where I buck up

my back for that is just not so. The Bible doesn't teach
that you are saved by faith only, and the man doesn't live
who can read that from God's divine will. The Bible says
we are saved by faith, but it doesn't say that we are saved
by faith alone, or by faith only. The Bible says we are
saved by grace, but the Bible doesn't say that we are
saved by grace ONLY. The Bible says we are saved by
hope, but it doesn't say we are saved by hope ONLY.
The Bible says we are saved by baptism, but it doesn't say
that we are saved by baptism ONLY. By what are we
saved? We are saved by everything to which God attributes salvation in the Bible, and that doesn't invalidate one
single solitary command that God has given. I could
write repentance up there on the blackboard, for surely
we are saved by repentance. We are saved by a multi-
plicity of things that have a direct bearing upon the subject. So don't you see that it is foolish for anyone to say,
"Oh, but I believe in salvation by the blood"? Well, bless
your soul, so do I. But I don't believe it is by blood ONLY,
that would cut out grace. I don't believe it is by faith ONLY,
that would cut out hope, the name, and all the things that
God says we are saved by. Therefore, you want to be careful
about that. Do you understand it? Now, friends, has
anybody got a question? If you want to ask me a question tonight, you can just stand up where you are; it is all
right with me. I am interested in teaching the truth because one day I am going to stand before a bigger audience than this and give an account unto my God for the
things that I say tonight, and the things I say every where
else I preach and I am preaching most of the time. What
I want to do, my friends, is to lead people to know the
truth and to understand the difference between truth and
error on these matters. Men are going about over the
country making a big noise about some of these things.
They are discounting the truths of God's divine will, and
when they do that they are bringing condemnation on the
souls of people—innocent victims of their teaching—and

it is my job and yours to try to lead those people to see the truth and that is what I am doing. I want to go to heaven myself, and I want you to go. I say those things kindly; I just want you to understand them, but it is my disposition to be emphatic about it. I am not mad at all, but I am sincere in what I am saying because God knows I want to be saved.

Well, I am going to preach a sermon tonight on the subject: *The Judgment Day.* I want to read from the 17th chapter of Acts as a background for some of the things that I want to present. Beginning with verse 29 the author says: "Forasmuch then as we are the offspring of God, we ought not to think that the Godhead is like unto gold, or silver, or stone, graven by art and man's device." You will remember Paul had just gone along there and had noted inscriptions of various kinds. In verse 30 he says: "And the times of this ignorance God winked at; but now commandeth all men every where to repent." Now you watch this: "Because he hath appointed a day, in the which he will judge the world in righteousness by that man whom he hath ordained; whereof he hath given assurance unto all men, in that he hath raised him from the dead." Now the point I want you to see is that he has appointed a day in which he will judge the world in righteousness by that man whom he hath ordained, namely: by the Lord Jesus Christ.

Judgment day, my friends, is something that we do not look forward to with any degree of joy or happy anticipation, but most of us consider judgment day as being something in the far distant future that we all dread. Well, I am sure that most intelligent people feel pretty much the same way about it, but there are some things about judgment day that you need to know, and I think as we study about it that you will be profited by the investigation. We are not talking about the fact that judgment is constantly before us. I sometimes preach a sermon on what I call "Three Tribunals." Man walks constantly before the tribunal of *Public Opinion.* You just can't ignore public opinion, but you have to recognize it, as to what people think about your life—what you are doing. You must consider that. You must be an example of good and right. Then second, you must pass before the tribunal of *Your Own Conscience* day by day. You have to live with yourself and your conscience is constantly judging you. And then there is number three, the *Final Judgment*. That is when we are before the Lord in judgment day that is coming eventually. Not only is that true, but there are some things about this that people do not understand. Great men have trembled, for instance, as recorded in Acts 24 and 25, at the thought of the judgment day. You are not by yourself if you feel that way about it. Listen to this: "And as he (Paul) reasoned of righteousness, temperance, and judgment to come, Felix trembled." The American Standard Version says: "Felix was terrified." No wonder he was terrified—no wonder he trembled. Paul was reasoning about righteousness, and he didn't know anything about righteousness; and about temperance, and he didn't understand the full meaning of temperature. But there was something about the judgment day that he could understand. As Paul reasoned about it, Felix trembled. You can say that the trembling was due to the coming of the judgment that Paul talked about. At least Paul convinced him that there is something terrible about that which is coming later, and that judgment is when you will stand before God and give an account for the deeds done in the body. There are a lot of other things we could bring up, but we are going to push them out of the way and get right down to the heart of the lesson.

First, I want to show you that judgment day is a day of absolute certainty. Listen to this: "And the time of this ignorance God winked at; but now commandeth all men every where to repent: because he hath appointed a day, in the which he will judge the world in righteousness by that man whom he hath ordained." Now then, the point is you had better repent of those things that you have done which are wrong, and the reason is because judgment day is coming. I want you to see this. The certainty of the coming of that day is taught, not only there, but also in the 9th chapter of Hebrews and verse 27: "And as it is appointed unto men once to die, but after this the judgment." The point is that sometime after death comes, you will be called from the grave to give an account unto God in the judgment. You don't know when judgment day is coming. In fact it is tied in with the second coming of Christ, and the Lord Jesus Christ said he didn't know when he was coming back. He said the angels in heaven do not know, only the Father knows, but the certainty of the judgment day is predicated upon the fact that God appointed it, even though you don't know when it is. Because of the certainty of the judgment, I think we ought to so live every day of our lives that no matter when it comes, we will be ready for it. Unless you are living when the Lord returns, you are going to die before the judgment day, and even those who are living will be changed in a moment, in the twinkling of an eye, at the last trump. The Bible says the trump will sound and the dead will rise, thus everybody gets up from the grave when the trump sounds, and very soon thereafter will be judged by the Lord Jesus Christ who comes with his angels bringing to those people who are unwilling to obey his will, eternal destruction. The certainty of that day, my brother, is important; and you ought to get right and ready for the judgment day, or the coming of death, because so far as you are concerned when you die then you have no other chance after death to get ready for the judgment day.

Somebody asked the question the other evening, What about praying for the dead? You remember the answer. When a man dies, he can not do anything about his future. He must do it all before he dies. Just as God has appointed that men will die, He has likewise appointed the fact that judgment day comes. There is death, that is appointed— the fact that men die is appointed; there is the judgment, that is likewise appointed. It is certain to come even though you do not know when it is coming. The point is: you had better be ready when judgment day arrives.

Let us notice another statement as we read that same passage one more time. He says: "He hath appointed a day in the which he will judge the world." Point number two: It is a day in which everybody is going to be there. Don't you worry about that, everybody is going to be there. I sometimes say that there are some things the Lord wants you to do that you must make a decision about. You make the decision, for example, as to whether you will hear God's word and obey His gospel. You make that decision. You make the decision as to whether, after you become a Christian, you will live the Christian life. That is your decision. But, brother, you don't have a decision with regard to death and the judgment. When you die, that is coming to you the same as to anybody else, and when you die you will receive the end of that which has been passed upon all men, and that is death. Everybody dies, and you don't have a choice in the matter. It is true that you can prolong your life by taking care of yourself, but one day you are going to die. The other thing is: you are going to come up from the grave and come to be judged before the Lord. You don't have a choice. You do have something to do about life. You may ignore God in this life if you choose, but you can't ignore Him when He calls you to come from the grave. In 2 Corinthians 5:10 he says: "For we must all appear before the judgment seat of Christ; that every one may receive the things done in his body, according to that he hath done, whether it be good or bad." Some people say the righteous are not coming into the judgment, that Christians, that saints, that godly people, that those who love the Lord, are going to be spared the judgment. Well, this passage says "whether they be good or bad."

Do you remember Jesus' judgment scene when he said he was going to separate them as a shepherd separated his sheep from the goats? And to those who are on the right hand, he will say, "Come ye blessed of my Father, inherit the kingdom prepared from the foundation of the world?" and while he is separating them, he will say to those on the left hand, "Depart into everlasting punishment, prepared for the devil and his angels." Now that is at the same time. Everybody is going to be there. That is one thing that you can be sure about. You can't get everybody to come to prayer meeting on Wednesday night, you can't get everybody out for the Sunday night service, you can't even get everybody to come to a revival meeting or a gospel meeting like this, but, brother, everybody is going to be present on judgment day! You don't have to worry about having to go and see them, you don't have to worry about the brethren and say: "Now come on, brother. You ought to be there you know, this is judgment day." No, that is not like prayer meeting night. You will not have to go get them or call them on the telephone. They are going to be there! The sad part of it is, a lot of them are not going to be ready.

Well, let us read another. In Revelation 1 and verse 4, John said that Christ would come, and in verse 7 he says: "Behold, he cometh with clouds; and every eye shall see him, and they also which pierced him: and all kindreds of the earth shall wail because of him. Even so, Amen." Now then, my third point is, that judgment day is a day of revelation. It is a day when the Lord will be revealed from heaven with his mighty angels, in flaming fire, taking vengeance on them that know not God, and obey not the gospel of our Lord Jesus Christ. Then another statement that I would like for you to notice is back in the Old Testament, in the book of Ecclesiastes 12:13,14: "Let us hear the conclusion of the whole matter: Fear God, and keep his commandments: for this is the whole duty of man. For God shall bring every work into judgment, with every secret thing, whether it be good, or whether it be evil." This is a day of revelation. I sometimes think of the misdeeds of people which are kept from the light of day. You don't know all about people; did you ever think about that? You may think you do. You don't even know your own husbands, some of you; you may not even know your own wives—I speak that respectfully of course. The point is that there are some things that we do not know about each other, but those things that we have not repented of, those acts that are still against us, are going to be brought into the judgment because the Bible says they are all going to be revealed, whether they are good or bad. Somebody brings up the absurd idea: "How in the world is the Lord Jesus Christ going to do all that on judgment day? Think of the millions and billions of people who have died as time has gone by." A lot of people think that they can make a problem so great that the Lord can not handle it. The fact of the matter is that God is equal to the task of anything that He sees fit to do. I don't know that God is going around doing things just to please people. Some years ago we used to have debates every Sunday afternoon in Washington, D. C. with the Catholics. The Catholic priest would speak for an hour and then he would answer questions or speak as long as he chose— maybe not an hour—then he would answer questions. His time came first, from 3:00 P.M. to 5:00 P.M. After he was through some of the preachers in the city would get up and preach a sermon, and we would stay there from 5:00 P.M. to 7:00 P.M., going over first one question and then another. Once in a while there would be an infidel or an agnostic or what have you, who would try to ask a question no one could answer. If you have even a little knowledge of the Bible, it is not too hard to just take the word of God and answer most of the silly questions that these people ask. The idea, for instance, where did Lot get his wife? And, Can God, if He can do everything, make a rock too big for Him to lift? Well, I am sure that God will use the same wisdom that He has manifested in everything else. So far as God being able to do something that He can't do is a contraction of terms. It not only puts him back where he started, but it is silly to start with. How then, is God going to do such a great thing as to have billions of people present on judgment day to judge them? It will be done the same way that God can know the hearts of these billions and billions of people. The Bible says He knows all about man. He knows what is in man. Now if He knows all that is in man, I have an idea that He can judge them on judgment day through the Lord Jesus Christ just like He said He would. Don't you worry about what God can do or what God can't do, brother; you had better worry about yourself, and whether or not you are ready when that time comes. Now here is the thought: judgment day is a day of revelation.

I want to read one more passage on this point: Romans 2:16. "In the day when God shall judge the secrets of men by Jesus Christ according to my gospel." The Bible says it is going to be according to my gospel, hence, this states the basis of judgment. But how is HE going to do this? Just like He does everything else. This judgment day is a day of revelation, and at that day of revelation men are going to be judged out of this book. I held this Book up before you the other evening, rather I propped it up here on the stand, and of course if I propped it up here now you could not see it for the flowers, but you couldn't read it if you could see it. This Book is going to be opened on the judgment day, at least for the sake of this illustration I am putting it that way. I don't know how the Lord is going to open the Book before them and judge them out of it, but He says that is the way it is going to be done. Let me read it for you. Revelation the 20th chapter, beginning at the last paragraph: "And I saw the dead, small and great, stand before God; and the books were opened: and another book was opened, which is the book of life: and the dead were judged out of those things which were written in the books, according to their works." The people who lived and died under the old dispensation will be judged according to the laws of that dispensation. You are living under the Christian dispensation; you are going to be judged by that dispensation. The thought that I want you to see is that it is a day of revelation, when you are going to be revealed and your secrets are going to be revealed and they are going to be judged by the will of God. Those things written will be the law by which you will be judged. John refers to it in John 20:30,31: "And many other signs truly did Jesus in the presence of his disciples, which are not written in this book: but these are written, that ye might believe that Jesus is the Christ, the Son of God; and that believing ye might have life through his name." People may say, "You don't have to pay any attention to what is written." You had better, brother, because the Bible says that these things that are written down are the things that you are to believe about the Lord and about his teaching; these are also the things you are going to be judged by. When you stand before him in the judgment you are going to be judged out of the things written in the Book and according to the things you have done.

I remember back in my early days as a boy when going to school, we used to go into the class room on examination day and the teacher would have on the desk a stack of mimeographed sheets, and we knew that was the examination. I would say to myself, "Oh, if I just could have had a copy of that to look over the night before, then I would know the answers, for if I just knew what the questions are I could look up the answers and have them ready." Do you know how I handle some of my classes out at Florida Christian College? I mimeograph the sheets and give them to the students the day before and let them take them home and look at them! Someone says, "My goodness, that is not a very good way to give an examination!" Yes it is. That is a pretty good way to give an examination; that is the way God does it. I am scriptural in that; that is the way God does it. He is giving you the examination questions. He has written them down for you in your language. You can see what He is going to require of you, and if you come up before Him and do not have the right answers, it is not going to mean that you will not get an "A"; it is going to mean that you are going to hell! You can understand that, and I want you to understand it. The examination questions that God is going to give is right here, (holds up the Bible) and in that day your deeds are going to be revealed and they are going to be judged by these examination questions that are found here. Now let me tell you something else: they are not in that little creed book that maybe you have been carrying around and reading, they are not in the prayer book, they are not in the church manual, they are in the New Testament. You had better quit reading the creed and read the New Testament, brother. You had better read God's word and find out what He wants you to do, because you are just as certain to be lost if you follow what man has said as you are seated in this building tonight. I want you to think about it.

But, I want you to notice about one or two more. In Matthew 7:21-23, we learn it is going to be a day of bitter regrets for some. "Not every one that saith unto me, Lord, Lord, shall enter into the kingdom of heaven; but he that doeth the will of my Father which is in heaven." Now here is the judgment day part of that: "Many will say to me in that day, Lord, Lord, have we not prophesied in thy name? and in thy name have cast out devils? and in thy name done many wonderful works? And then will I profess unto them, I never knew you: depart from me, ye that work iniquity."

"Do you mean that you never knew me, Lord, after all that I did? Why I was a member of the biggest church in town, I had my name on the biggest membership-roll in my city, and you mean that you don't know me?"

This is sort of like the fellow one time, you know, that was worrying about the fact that they wouldn't take him into a certain church. He had a dream that night and he dreamed that he was talking to the Lord. The Lord said to him: "Son, don't worry about it; I haven't been able to get into that church either." So you have your name on the biggest church in town; so you have been prophesying, teaching in the name of the Lord? Well, that is all fine but the Lord said, I never knew you.

"Why don't you know me, Lord, I have been doing all these things?"

"Well, you depart from me, ye that work iniquity, I never knew you; you didn't do my will.

"Why did not you know me?"

Let me read the paragraph above. He said: "I don't know you because you didn't do my will." It is not the one who says, Lord, Lord, but it is the one who "does the will of the Father." Wouldn't you hate to live out your life, zealous and active in something that you thought was right, as the ones Paul mentions in Romans 10:1: "For I bear them record that they have a zeal of God, but not according to knowledge?" Thus they are going about to establish their own righteousness, not knowing the righteousness of God, and will be lost. Wouldn't you hate to do that ? I would. I would hate to live out my life and then come before the Lord in judgment and have him say to me, "Yes, you wore a denominational name," and the Bible says in Acts 4:12: "There is none other name under heaven given among men, whereby we must be saved," therefore, "depart from me." The Bible teaches that you must do His will, that you must wear His name, that you must follow his teaching, and it is not complicated or difficult. Thus, my friends, it is going to be a day of grave and serious regret for those who are not obedient to him."

My father was not a child of God. I used to hear him say time and time again when I would preach to him trying to get him to see that he was lost, "Now Harry, don't you worry about me. Don't you worry about me, son, I am all right."

I would say to him, "But you haven't obeyed Christ."

He would say, "I don't believe Christ was necessarily the Son of God. I don't believe the Bible is the Word of God, that is the reason."

One day my father is going to come before the judgment bar of God, just like your father, and my mother, and everybody's father and mother. My father is going to come before the judgment of God, but, brother, I want to tell you: God is no respecter of persons, whether it is your mother and father or my mother and father. It is based upon whether or not that person has done the will cf God or not. My daddy is going to have some terrible regrets in the judgment because he died out of Christ, disbelieving in the Lord and disbelieving in the Bible as the inspired word of God. I have shed many tears over the grave of my mother and father. They are now sleeping side by side in the Spring Hill Cemetery just outside of Nashville, Tennessee. I never visit that city but that I go out there and stand by the grave; but my tears are to no avail. I could shed an ocean of tears but I couldn't change the spiritual condition of my parents—or anyone else. Listen, brother: judgment day is going to be a day of deep regrets. It is going to be a day of the severing between the families of the earth, where mother, father, brother and sister are divided because of their failure to obey God's will.

Finally, friends, listen to this: It is going to be a day of great rejoicing. I Peter 4:13. "But rejoice, inasmuch as ye are partakers of Christ's sufferings; that, when his glory shall be revealed, ye may be glad also with exceeding joy." Matthew 25:34. "Come, ye blessed of my Father, inherit the kingdom prepared for you from the foundation of the world." Judgment day! You had better not throw this thing around, you had better not treat it lightly, you had better not say to yourself: "Pickup is just agitated about this thing. He is upset about it." Yes, I am; yes, I am. Because people are being lost. They are out of Christ. There will be a judgment day, a day of deep regret, a day of great rejoicing. Oh, if I can just hear my name called, "Come, ye blessed of my Father." If I can just hear the Lord say to me: "Come up higher into the home that I have prepared for you," I will be mighty happy.

I preached the funeral of the daughter of John Vanderver who lives, or did in in Madisonville, Tennessee, just north of Nashville.   The baby was four years old. The mother and father, in talking to me about the arrangements of the funeral, said: "We would like for you to preach the funeral of this baby, and we want the quartet to sing *There Is A Great Day Coming*."   That is the song you sang just a little while ago.   *There Is A Great Day Coming*.   Well, I said to them: "Why that song?"   John Vanderver said, "Harry, the little girl was very fond of that song.   She used to go about the house singing the song: 'There's a Great Day Coming, There's a Great Day Coming.'"   Now she didn't realize the significance of it, but you and I do.   As we all sat there the quartet sang: "There's A Great Day Coming."

Friends, there is a great day coming, and it is coming when the Lord shall sound his trumpet, when the dead shall rise and when you are called to stand before Christ in the judgment.   The important thing is, will you be ready?

"There's a great day coming, A great day coming,
   There's a great day coming by and by;
   When the saints and the sinners shall be parted right
      and left,
   Are you ready for that day to come?"

Believe His word, obey His gospel, put Him on in baptism and live faithfully unto death.   Will you respond tonight while we stand and sing?

SPIRITUAL HEART TROUBLE

We are grateful for your presence tonight and hope that you get some blessing out of my part of the service. I trust that you will come as often as possible and study with us the lessons that we present from evening to evening. As Brother Phillips announced, we have been answering questions when those questions have been turned in. We have had several, and he handed me some more since I came into the building tonight. I don't usually answer questions unless I have had some time to think them over, but I am going to at least make an attempt to answer these tonight in view of the fact that possibly the ones who asked them would like for them to be answered tonight. Now I don't know whether that is so or not, but I will do the best that I can and move as rapidly as possible, because I have a habit of preaching a long time anyhow and I don't want to take too much time with the questions, but enough time to give the best answer that I can.

Here is the first one: "Are all Old Testament prophecies fulfilled?" Well, I would say yes, all that were supposed to be fulfilled in the coming of Christ, and the various other things that happened during the New Testament dispensation. Those that were not—those that had reference to time that is yet the future—we would, of course, say, have not been fulfilled. I don't know just how to answer that unless it be along that line. For instance, one of the passages of Scripture that I used from the Old Testament last evening: "For God will bring every work into judgment, with every secret thing, whether it be good or evil." is a prophecy concerning the last day, or the day when God will bring all things into the judgment. Well, obviously that has not been fulfilled; it has reference to time yet in the future. If he is talking about the final judgment when all things are brought into that judgment and the secrets of men's hearts are made open, then that prophecy has not been fulfilled. Now if you mean many of the things that some people think are yet in the future, then of course the individual prophecy would have to be considered. I think, for example, that God has already completed all the promises that He gave to the Jews, and yet many people think that God is going to restore them to Palestine, that there are prophecies to that effect. God has fulfilled every prophecy or promise that He made to them. I believe that in Christ Jesus all spiritual promises to all nations have been fulfilled. When He promised to give them the land, He kept that one. Joshua tells us that it all came to pass, Joshua 21:43-45. The restoration promise came to pass when God restored Israel to her native land. Of course I would have to know the individual prophecy which the writer of the question had in mind, and I don't know this, so that is the way I will have to answer it.

Now here is another one that deals with a very difficult problem that I could spend a lot of time on and maybe still not get the answer. "What is the difference between the sin unto death in John 5:16 and blasphemy against the Holy Spirit in Matthew 12:31?" I am going to read these statements rapidly and get the thought before you as best I can. In the book of Matthew, 13th chapter and verse 31: "Wherefore I say unto you, All manner of sin and blasphemy shall be forgiven unto me: but the blasphemy against the Holy Ghost shall not be forgiven unto them. And whosoever speaketh a word against the Son of man, it shall be forgiven him: but whosoever speaketh against the Holy Ghost, it shall not be forgiven him, neither in this world, neither in the world to come." I have heard the statements that men make about that, that this sin is a peculiar sin in that it is against the Holy Spirit—that this sin is like a lot of other things that people do against the Holy Spirit, and you can commit that sin in various ways. It is my understanding of it, friends, that the sin against the Holy Spirit as the Lord describes it is where somebody attributes to Satan the work of God. Now if that isn't it, then I just don't understand the language. Well, what is it? Jesus said it was the sin or blasphemy against the Holy Spirit. What is that? It is attributing unto the Devil or to the forces of evil that which is done by God. For example, Jesus was casting out demons, and they said, You are doing that by Beelzebub. Jesus said, I am not doing anything of the sort; it is not by Beelzebub. If Satan's house is divided against him, that is what I would be doing and it would be wrong. The sin against the Holy Spirit, undoubtedly, had something to do with the fact that men were attributing unto the Devil the work of the Lord.

Now somebody says, Can it be performed today? Well, I just don't know. I know I hear sermons preached on the Sin Against The Holy Spirit. It simply boils down to the fact that when you resist the word of God that you are committing the sin against the Holy Spirit and that is all there is to it, but I never have thought that was it. Of course, I could be mistaken about what I am saying with reference to it. My thought is that it is attributing unto the Devil the power of the Lord Jesus Christ. Well, let us see how this fits in with the statement over here in I John. John is saying in this passage, the 5th chapter and verse 16: "If any man see his brother sin a sin which is not unto death, he shall ask, and he shall give him life for them that sin not unto death. There is a sin unto death: I do not say that he shall pray for it. All unrighteousness is sin:" then he said: "and there is a sin not unto death." Now if there is a sin not unto death, and a sin unto death, then, concerning the sin unto death, he said, don't pray for the man that you see committing it. Well, what is it? I don't think it is the sin against the Holy Spirit, to be perfectly frank with you. I want to turn back and read a statement in the first chapter of I John. In the 8th verse he says "If we say that we have no sin, we deceive ourselves, and the truth is not in us. If we confess our sins, he is faithful and just to forgive us our sins, and to cleanse us from all unrighteousness. If we say that we have not sinned, we make him a liar, and his word is not in us." Now then, what does that amount to? If I see a man sinning a sin, and he stubbornly refuses to confess his fault, and I know that is the condition, could I go to my heavenly

Father and say, "Oh, Father, now I'll tell you what I want
you to do: my brother over here is sinning, and although
he knows that he has committed sin and is too hard-headed
to confess it (he has an advocate with the Father if he will
confess his sins, but he will not do that), I pray that thou
will forgive that fellow his sins regardless of what he does."
I never do pray that God will forgive a man from his sins
as long as that fellow is continuing in sin and stubbornly
refuses to do God's will. I pray that God will show him
the way, and that he will turn away from his unrighteousness, but I can't pray for God to forgive him unless he
does turn. We say: "Father, forgive us our sins as we
forgive those who sin against us." But I can't pray God to
forgive your sins if you are stubbornly refusing to do God's
will and are continuing in that sin. I can see that; I can
see that kind of sin because the Bible refers to it. When
an individual commits a sin that he will not confess, even
though God promises if we confess our sins then He will
forgive us, do you suppose that I could pray for God to
forgive him? No, I could not. Now I don't know whether
or not that fully answers the question, but I don't think the
two sins are the same thing. They may be. There may be
a sense in which they are but I don't think they are the
same thing.

Now the last question: "What does the Bible say about
second marriages?" Well, there are several things the Bible
says about them, and I will read some of them and make a
little comment and pass on. In Matthew the 19th chapter
and beginning at verse 9, the people asked Jesus a question
one day and he replied to it. He said: "Whosoever shall
put away his wife, except it be for fornication, and shall
marry another, committeth adultery: and whoso marrieth
her which is put away doth commit adultery." The fellow
marries another; that is the second marriage. Then over
here in I Corinthians 7 and beginning at verse 39: "The
wife is bound by the law as long as her husband liveth;
but if her husband be dead, she is at liberty to be married
to whom she will; only in the Lord." Now that is a sec-

ond marriage too. There are two cases of second marriages. In other words, a second marriage can be engaged in:

1. Provided the husband or wife of this individual is dead.

2. It can be engaged in provided the divorce or separation is based upon the adultery or the unfaithfulness of the companion that is being put away.

In other words, it is REALLY a case of adultery. I don't mean that they can separate for something other than adultery and then finally one of the parties commits adultery and the other can claim this gives him the freedom that he has been expecting. Fornication was not the cause of the putting away in that case at all. The cause was the fact that they just couldn't get along together—incompatibility (that covers a multitude of sins along that line). What was the reason for the divorce? Simply the fact that they couldn't get along. I heard of a couple out in Memphis, Tennessee a few years ago who fell out over a jar of pickles, and got a divorce, by the way. That was the cause, and both of them admitted it so I understand. They married again. Now that is a second marriage. Jesus teaches that the divorce in the case he is talking about is based upon the fact that one party has been unfaithful or has been disloyal by committing adultery. What does that do? I think that releases the innocent party. If that isn't what Jesus is teaching, I don't know what he is talking about.

Well, how about the one over here in the book of I Corinthians? It says if this woman's husband be dead, then she is at liberty to be married in the Lord. I know that sometimes people say, "Well, I don't think there is too much importance to be placed upon that fact." I just know lots of people that don't practice that part of it. Here is a member of the church, her husband dies and she decides to get married again, she just marries the first fellow who pops the question. Of course, maybe that is not the way it ought to be put, but, anyhow, she gets married pretty

soon. She doesn't even stop to think whether the person
is a Christian or not. If I know anything about the language at all, and I am certainly not an authority on it, I
think this refers to the fact that "in the Lord" means this
man is a Christian. She may be married to whom she will,
if she marries a Christian. All right, what about second
marriages? Second marriages, if the wife's husband is
dead, she may be married again, only in the Lord. What
about the other second marriage? If adultery is the cause
of the separation, then Jesus Christ states that the relationship with the new companion is legitimate, based upon
his statement in the 19th chapter of Matthew. Now if that
isn't it, then I am certain that I don't know what is the
meaning of it.

Tonight I want to speak for a little while (and I hope
it will be a little while and not as long as it was last night)
on a statement that is made in the 14th chapter of John.
I want you to listen carefully as I read a statement that
you have heard at funerals all your life. When a preacher
stands up at a funeral you just know he is going to read
this passage of Scripture. "Let not your heart be troubled:
ye believe in God, believe also in me. In my Father's house
are many mansions: if it were not so, I would have told
you. I go to prepare a place for you. And if I go and prepare a place for you, I will come again, and receive you
unto myself; that where I am, there ye may be also."

Now, friends, my point tonight is based upon the first
verse: *Heart Trouble!* He says, "Let not your heart be
troubled." Now I don't anymore think that the Lord gave
that expression for people to use at funerals, necessarily,
than that he gave it to be read at weddings. I think the
passage has a direct application to the lives of those disciples. The Lord was about to leave them, and while there
is that connection with a funeral, I believe he is talking
about something that goes a lot deeper than that. He said:
"Let not your heart be troubled." "It is true that I am
going away, but believe in God and that will cure your
trouble; believe in God and believe in me." Then he said,

"In my Father's house are many mansions." My point is: spiritual heart trouble has to do with something that we find mentioned in the Bible many times, and it is a disease that is extremely serious.

I want you to notice the statement that is made concerning the heart as is referred to in Matthew the 9th chapter and the 4th verse. He says: "As a man thinketh in his heart, so is he." Then over here in Romans the 10th chapter and 10th verse: "With the heart man believeth unto righteousness, and with the mouth confession is made unto salvation." In Romans the 10th chapter and the 1st verse: "My heart's desire and prayer to God for Israel is, that they might be saved." In 2 Corinthians the 9th chapter and the 7th verse: "As a man purposeth in his heart, so let him give." What is he talking about? He says the heart is that with which one purposes; that is, he makes his plans with his heart, or with his mind. He is talking about the thing with which he thinks—"As a man thinketh in his heart, so is he." It is the thing with which he desires. There are many similar expressions found in the Bible that refer to the heart.

Now, friends, that is the thing that gets wrong with man. It is not the fact that he has a heart disease such as a physical heart ailment, but I am making the application of the expressions used in the Bible to show that they refer to a spiritual condition. Here is a spiritual heart trouble, a trouble that people have because their hearts are wrong in some way, and I want to describe that tonight. But I want you to see that the heart is the mind of man. Someone says, "Why does he use 'heart' when he should have used the expression 'mind' instead?" Well, I don't know why that the Holy Sprit saw fit to put it that way except for the fact that it indicates that which man purposes, with which man thinks, with which man desires and so on; that is, it is not necessarily referring to his emotions when we say the heart. We usually mean the emotions of man when we use that expression. I think that is so with the average use of the expression or term, and also we use the heart as the Bible uses it with regard to the mind, or with regard to the intellect or intelligence that man employs in his various activities, either in the church or out of the church. Now I want to talk along that line tonight, and I want you to see that I am talking about that rather than about the emotions of man altogether.

First of all I want to read a passage from the 13th chapter of Matthew that refers to a spiritual heart trouble that he calls a "gross heart." Listen to this: "For this people's heart is waxed gross." That "waxed gross" is "epachunthe." (By the way, my Greek teacher is here tonight and I want to show off). "The People's heart is waxed gross, and their ears are dull of hearing, and their eyes have they closed; lest at any time they should see with their eyes, and hear with their ears, and should understand with their heart, and should be converted, and I should heal them." There is the explanation the Lord makes regarding a heart that he refers to as a "gross heart." What is a "gross heart"? I have jotted it down here on the margin of my notes. Thayer says it means "to be rendered calloused and unfeeling," or as we sometimes say "thick." Did you ever refer to an individual as "fat headed"? That is an expression that could well be applied to having a gross heart. I mean that it represents a dullness that is based upon the WILLINGNESS of the individual to become dull or listless, and to be calloused and unfeeling. The Lord said that they are dull and listless. Not only is that true, but he said this people's heart is waxed gross, "and their ears have they closed." In other words, the closing of the ears to the truth, the closing of the eyes to the truth, the closing of the mind to the truth, God describes in the Bible as a heart that is gross. I think it is different from the "hard heart," I am going to talk about a little later. I believe, while it is a willing state of mind, it is something that is perfectly acceptable to the individual. He says, "Lest at any time they should see with their eyes." Does he mean that the people are really blinding themselves, actually and literally in order that they might not see?

No. He is referring to a condition of their minds. Their minds were blinded, and he uses that figure of speech to show that their minds had been closed. They may have literally closed their eyes, I don't know. I have seen people that would literally close their eyes to truths that were actually pointed out to them and would refuse to read exactly what God says.

I remember that some time ago in a religious discussion, a man tried to get another man to stand up and actually read what God said about a thing, and he wouldn't do it. Now what is that? Well, you might say that fellow is hard hearted, or it could be a gross heart that will refuse to examine the evidence based upon a listlessness, a dullness that was due to some circumstances that had entered into his life. I want you to notice this statement once more. He says: "Lest," that is, for fear or "in order that," they might see with their eyes, and that they might be prevented from hearing with their ears and understanding with their hearts and should be converted. This perhaps has one thing about it that is worse than anything else, that is the willingness on the part of the individual to accept such a situation as that. Do you know anybody like that? Do you know any person that is in that condition due to the fact that he listlessly and in a dull manner refuses to accept truth, not because he is especially hard hearted, but he has turned away his ears from hearing it so long that his mind has become calloused and listless about the truth?

I can't help but notice people when I preach, in fact I think it is my business to notice people when I preach. I always did hate to see a preacher preach to the corner of the room up yonder, then turn over here and preach up to the corner of the room over here. I like to see a fellow look me in the eye when he talks to me. If I am out in the congregation I want him to look at me. In looking at people as you preach to them you get an idea of how they are responding, or whether they are responding at all to what you say. There is a church member I preach to occasionally

who, of all the people I can think of, at least right now—
maybe I could think hard and think of somebody that would
be her equal—of all the people that I can think of right now
on the spur of the moment, that person it seems to me, is
about as "gross of heart" as any person that I know. She
will close her eyes when I am making as much noise as I
am right now and doze in my face. I think her heart is
GROSS; I think she has willingly allowed herself to slip
into that predicament. I believe her heart is gross, not
because she sleeps in public, but because of the fact that
the circumstances of her life indicate a dullness of mind,
spiritually speaking, which has stiffled her interest in godly
things.

But I turn to another passage. In Hebrews the 3rd
chapter and beginning at verse 8 I want to talk to you
about the "hard" or disobedient, unbelieving heart. I think
all three of these terms, perhaps, describe the same thing.
I know that is the way it is used here. The writer of the
book of Hebrews says: "Harden not your hearts, as in
the provocation, in the day of temptation in the wilderness:
when your fathers tempted me, proved me, and saw my
works forty years. Wherefore I was grieved with that
generation, and said, They do always err in their heart;
and they have not known my ways. So I sware in my
wrath, They shall not enter into my rest." Now here is
his application of the Old Testament example. "Take heed,
brethren, lest there be in any of you an evil heart of unbelief, in departing from the living God." Paul said that
those Israelites had "erred in their hearts." Now what
was the trouble with them? He said that their hearts were
hard. Now he describes that as unbelieving, as erring
hearts: hearts that had erred from the truth. He goes on
and points out that they have erred through their unbelief.
Now what had they done? Let me read it again. He says
that they had not followed God's way. That is one thing,
but we see them, not only not following God's way, but
stubbornly TURNING AWAY from the way of God. Then
he says that they had done it in unbelief. That is HARD

HEARTED. Hard in the sense that the individual has turned away from God. You know, to me that is a methodical, planned procedure. Paul says, Brethren, be sure that no wicked heart of unbelief may come into you, into your hearts or into your lives.

Let us notice another thing about that. How could we possibly get into such a condition today? Well, I think by a refusal to do God's will. I understand that people are sometimes uneducated with regard to the word of God. One of the things that the Lord taught against about as much as anything in the world was stupidity. I think that is the way he uses the word "foolish." The "foolish" man that built his house upon the sand, was a "stupid" man. The "stupid" man built his house upon the sand; the rains descended, the floods came, the winds blew and beat upon that house. Well, who built it? A stupid fellow, a foolish man. Another "stupid" man tore down his barns and built larger barns. The individual who has gotten into such a condition as is here described because of his unwillingness to follow the way of the Lord may be one with a hard heart. I have heard of people of whom it was said that they actually removed certain statements from their Bibles because they didn't believe them. They refused to accept them because they were not pleasant to them, thus turning away in that sense. This kind also is voluntary. I remember a few years ago an example that I have read somewhere, maybe in one of the books by one of the Lipscombs, and it concerns one of the great pioneer preachers who had been preaching out in the western part of the state of Tennessee. Brother F. D. Srygley, I believe it was, had been preaching in a certain community for many years. Every year he had gone back to that same place until he had been there, as I remember the example, twenty times. The first time he was there an individual came there and he enjoyed hearing that great man preach. He almost obeyed the gospel at that first service, but day by day and year by year as he heard the gospel, he determined to turn himself away from it. He didn't have the right attitude toward it, and eventually when the last series of meetings was over, Brother F. D. Srygley said that fellow came down the aisle after the sermon was over, after the prayer had been said, after the people were going out of the building, and he said in substance: "Mr. Srygley, while I enjoyed your discussion tonight, it made no impression upon my heart whatsoever!" No impression! I think that fellow had hardened his heart.

I remember a few years ago over in a neighboring state the preacher of a local congregation asked me to come over and help them to settle a trouble in the church. I went over there and tried to help them get the matter settled, and everyone was in a pretty good humor except one fellow. You know, I am a very agreeable individual and want to get along with everybody, and do. But sometimes you find somebody that you just can't get along with to save your life. This individual was unwilling to listen to reason, and I went at it in every way that I possibly could. I said: "My good brother, you will see that this thing is hurting the church, why can't you just forgive this person?" It involved one of his own flesh. I said: "She has admitted that she has made a mistake; she has asked on bended knee that you forgive her. Why can't you break your will and bow your stubborn heart to this situation and get right in the matter?" When I said that, he just patted his mouth and said nothing. What kind of a heart is that? Hard hearted! A man can put his fingers to his ears in order to prevent his hearing something that he needs to know about his own condition, or he can refuse to act even though he hears. It is the same either way. He has a hard, calloused heart. If a man is going to so turn away his heart and so harden himself that he will refuse to hear, I don't know what you can do with him except to turn him over to the devil. That may not make any impression on him either, but there is nothing else to do. Now, friends, I will tell you what I want you to do. You may not agree with some of the preaching that has been done in this meeting, I don't know whether you do or not. It may be that everybody here believes it and agrees with it; I hope so. I mean I hope you agree with what God teaches whether you agree with my manner of presentation or not; I hope that you appreciate and understand it and are trying your best to follow the will of the Lord. I want you to take everything that God says which concerns you, and think the matter through with an open mind. Study it in the light of God's will.

I have known people who hardened their hearts against the church of the New Testament. I actually had a lady tell me one time: "I don't like the way you use the expression, 'the church of the New Testament' because I can just tell by the way you use it that you mean that everybody else is wrong." I said, "Sister, I am mighty glad you got the point." This thing is right, brother! (holding up the Bible). I may not be, but this is. Take the church for example: The Bible says, and the Lord Jesus Christ himself said: "Upon this rock I will build my church." Now that is not a denomination; that is the church of the New Testament. The Lord is the author of the expression and when I use it, I am speaking correctly. It IS the church about which you can read in the New Testament. You get out the denominational manual, or the creed book, or the prayer book or what ever you use, and try to read some of the denominational expressions which you and others use. Now don't get mad, just read them. I used to attend the Baptist church—Park Avenue Baptist Church out in West Nashville, Tennessee many years ago. I was never a member of it, but I attended its services. I went there for many years, was in the Sunday School, and had a big time at all the picnics and just got along fine. In fact, I was coming along right well. I heard a gospel sermon on the church of the New Testament. Well, I said that was a Baptist Church, or it may be a Methodist Church. I have attended the Methodist Church, and some of the best friends I have are members of the Methodist Church and the Baptist Church, the Episcopal Church and even the Roman Catholic Church. I have some very fine friends in

all these churches. Now here is my point: It doesn't make
any difference whether you agree with what I say or not,
that is beside the point. You open your Book and see what
IT says about any matter. Suppose you are going to study
the matter of the church? What does the Bible say about
the church? Now you just think of your denominational
concept of it and you study that angle of it, and you say
to yourself: "Where does the Bible teach these various
things that we are doing, the practices in which we engage? You study that with an open mind, an open heart,
not just pitching the thing over your shoulder and saying:
"Well!!" Take the subject of baptism. What does the
Bible teach us on it? You say, "I have gone over that time
and time again but I just don't like it. I have been prac-
ticing sprinkling for baptism all of my days and I just don't
like the idea of something else. You can't tell me that a
preacher like Harry Pickup knows more about it than all
of these great men that are in the world." Did it ever
occur to you that there are some "great" men in the world
who believe the ideals of Communism? You tell me that
we should use the standard of great men? Just because of
the fact that a fellow happens to be "great" and has a lot
of medals, or has gone to a lot of universities and has a
great many degrees, is that absolute reason to follow him?
Do you suppose authority is based upon such? NO, friends!
It is based on what God says about it, not whether a man
is great or not great. You just forget men in this matter
and look at the Lord and what He says in His teaching.
Here is the thought that I want you to get in all this: don't
harden your heart; don't worry about men. Just open your
Bible and read what it teaches concerning that on which
you are a little ruffled. If it is the church, then read about
the church; if it is the name, then read about the name;
if it is baptism, then read about baptism. Whatever it is
just open the Book and read—I mean this Book (holding
up the Bible), not the creed book, but the New Testament.
And then, don't harden your heart; don't turn away and
say: "Well, I just can't accept it," but read it and study

it and let your heart be open to the reception of the truth, even though you haven't accepted it, open your heart and study the matter.

I will get on to another one. In Matthew 15:18-20 Jesus says: "But those things which proceed out of the mouth come from the heart; and they defile the man. For out of the heart proceed evil thoughts, murders, adulteries, fornications, thefts, false witness, blasphemies: these are the things which defile a man: but to eat with unwashen hands defileth not a man." Now what is that? (Writes on blackboard) I hope that is the correct spelling of it; if it isn't, it is supposed to be IMMORAL. *An Immoral Heart!* What is an immoral heart! The Lord said it was a heart out of which proceeded immoral things, immoral activities, immoral imaginations, immoral concepts of life. You can just think about things and become immoral. That is the reason the Lord said in the great sermon on the mount, "Whoso is angry with his brother without a cause" has violated God's law. The law said, "Thou shalt not kill," but what is the great difference between the law of Moses and the law of Christ with regard to murder? One deals with the overt act; the other deals with the thinking about murder—the being angry enough to kill. Don't ever get angry enough to take a life; that is the thinking the Lord condemns. He said with respect to adultery, The law says not to commit adultery, but I say don't even look upon a woman to lust after her in your heart because you will commit adultery in your heart if you do. The heart is the thing that is concerned with immorality: an immoral heart. Out of the heart are the issues of life, and that individual's heart, which is immoral, will think immoral things and will act in an immoral way.

Then I could mention the 5th chapter of Acts and verses 1 to 4, where we have the hypocritical hearts of Ananias and Sapphira. In the 8th chapter of Acts and verse 18 we have a covetous heart on the part of Simon the sorcerer. Time will not allow that I discuss every one, so I want to bring the sermon to a conclusion with the thoughts

that I have presented already. What causes the gross
heart, the hard heart and the immoral heart, or whatever
heart trouble that you may have of a spiritual nature?

I want to look in a passage in the Old Testament first
of all. In Joshua 7:5: "Wherefore the hearts of the people
melted, and became as water." There is a melting heart
that is brought about by weakness. Listen, friends, I think
maybe all these begin in that way. These is a sense in
which the gross heart may be attributed to the weakness
of that individual. Now we turn over here to one in the
New Testament, the 12th chapter of Hebrews where Paul
says, "For consider him that endured such contradiction
of sinners against himself, lest ye be wearied and faint in
your minds." Then he says, "For in due season we shall
reap if we faint not." That is one of the causes of this
heart trouble, the fact that people faint in their hearts.
First they are weak, then they faint, and there is another.
I now read from the Book of Hosea 10:2 where Hosea
says: "Their heart is divided." Dividing the affections
will bring about spiritual heart trouble. Now watch: There
is weakness, there is fainting and there is division that
could bring about any of these things. They could even
cause the heart to become fat, to become grossed, to become calloused and unfeeling. Unfeeling is actually brought
about by either weakness, fainting or dividing or turning
away from the truth of God and a steeling of one's self
against the principles of right.

I remember a few years ago in a meeting, one of the
first meetings that I conducted, I came upon an individual
who set herself against the truth for years. I had preached
in about two meetings in that community prior to this incident. There was a lady that lived in the community
just a stone's throw from the church building, and she
came, as I remember, to almost every service. She had
several children and relatives who had also attended the
meeting. One by one many of those relatives came and
confessed Christ, were buried in baptism for the remission
of their sins and arose to walk the new life. The last night

of the last meeting that she attended I was standing on one side of the door and the song leader was standing on the other side of the door—it was a big wide door, plenty of room to pass between us. The song leader would shake hands with people over there and I would shake hands with people over here, telling them goodbye, the last night of the meeting. This lady, when she came out of the door that night, I never shall forget, had sort of a smirk on her face. She said: "Well, you didn't get me." The song leader, Brother T. A. Nicks, a great man, a wonderful song leader, said: "Mother"—she was a woman of 55 or perhaps 60—"we didn't come down here to get you, but I want to tell you, if you don't change your ways and obey God the devil is going to get you." What had happened to that lady? Just a continual growth of a combination of weakness, a fainting heart and the disposition to turn away from the word until her heart had hardened against the truth of the gospel. That is what caused it.

Now, friends, what is the remedy? Well, I'll tell you. I want to get right back to the passage that I started with. "In my Father's house are many mansions," Jesus said. "I am going away and coming back but don't have any heart trouble while I am gone." How are we going to prevent it? BELIEF: "believe in God, believe also in me." How are you going to remedy a gross heart? The answer is FAITH. That is what Jesus said. He said: "Let not your heart be troubled." Don't let your hearts be troubled or be afraid, "believe in God, believe also in me." Faith is the remedy for the kind of heart trouble the Lord is talking about. What will faith do to a gross heart? Why faith will cause that gross heart to open, if it will only allow faith to come in. The Bible says that faith comes by hearing and hearing by the word of God. So when faith, that comes by hearing, enters the heart of that individual, the mind, the intellect, the intelligence of that person grasps the truths and the heart opens. You can't keep a heart gross where faith is. If the heart is hard the only thing in the world that will break that thing down is faith. Faith in God will do it; faith in Christ, faith in the Bible. The only thing that will correct the immoral heart is faith. "Believe in God, believe also in me." Now, friends, the faith that will do the bidding of the Lord is what I mean. Not an inactive faith; not a faith that doesn't move according to the principles of truth; but a faith that will say, "Lord, lead me by thy Holy Word and I'll do your bidding." That kind of faith will cure those kinds of heart trouble or any other kind of heart trouble.

Friends, do you believe in God—in Christ? If so, I will tell you what to do. If you believe in Him and have wondered about your condition, or if you have thought about the state of your soul or the condition of your soul, then let that faith lead you to examine the record. Then just start reading to let God tell you just what He wants you to do about it. Don't read your Bible with the idea of "How can I justify myself in my position?" That is not the way to read the Bible. Read the Bible with faith. Open the Book and say, "Lord, what do you want me to know about this subject?" Whatever it might be, study it with the heart, the understanding, with the intellect, with the mind. Put your mind on it and if your heart has become gross or calloused, or immoral, or covetous, or if you have been wayward and negligent and indifferent, or if you have sinned against God, then correct your heart trouble by faith. Have faith to believe His word and follow His will. If your heart is hard, then faith can open it if you will let it. When you hear His word and understand it, then do something about your condition.

Are you here tonight out of Christ? Are you a member of the church that you can read about in that Book? If you are not, you ought to be. If you are not a member of the church that you can read about in that Book, then I am urging you tonight to let your whole soul be concerned with the gospel of Christ by believing His word; turn away from error and sin, confess Jesus before men, and then be buried in baptism for the remission of your sins, because that is what the Bible teaches that men did then to become

members of that church. You will not have to join anything because as the Book says, the Lord will add you to
the family of God and the church of the New Testament.
Will you obey the gospel? If you are out of duty, why
don't you come home tonight? Believe His word and let it
have free course in your life by saying to yourself: "I am
sorry for my negligence; I am sorry that I have been wayward and indifferent; I am sorry for my backsliding and
I repent of them and I will confess my faults and backsliding." We will pray with and for you and God says He
will heal you. If you are subject of the invitation why
will you not come tonight while we together stand and
sing?

QUESTIONS AND ANSWERS

Once again it is our purpose and desire to speak to you about things that concern our eternal welfare, and to guide this survey of Truth as God has presented that Truth in His Holy Will. I want to speak tonight on some of the questions that God may ask you at the judgment. We have talked to you about the judgment; we have discussed on numerous occasions the plan of salvation, the truths that God has presented in His word for men to follow today, and tonight we want to try and draw some conclusions from things that were asked individuals in Bible times. These are questions that either God or a representative of God asked to some human being. Not only are the questions significant, my friends, but the answers are also significant. As the question is propounded by God or one of His representatives, and the answer is given, there is a deep significance attached to both the questions and the answers.

The asking and answering of questions has always been an effective way of teaching the truth. Even Jesus used that method, and although he was divine and understood all the ways that would be effective in reaching people, frequently he would answer a question by asking one. There were many questions propounded to the Lord that were not important, doubtless, at least the Lord dismissed them with an answer which showed that there was no special importance connected with them. For instance, they asked him: "Whose wife shall she be in the resurrection?" The Lord replied that "there is no marrying nor giving in marriage in the resurrection." There were many other times that the people came, especially the scribes and the Pharisees, to trap him or catch him in talk. That method has been employed by good men and by bold adversaries of right in presenting their various points of view. We are concerned tonight, my friends, with some of the things that God may ask you, and He may ask me in the judgment, because He did ask individuals in the days past and gone. Without any further emphasis upon that angle of it, I would like for us to consider some of the things God did actually ask individuals on this earth. I am going, first of all, to the Old Testament, back to the very beginning of the Bible, in Genesis 3:9. We find there that man was hiding from the presence of God among the trees of the garden. You remember that man had walked and talked with God prior to this in a very friendly fashion, almost as one man to another, but now because sin has entered the life of this man and his wife, they are hiding themselves among the trees of the garden, as the voice of God came down to them once again. Here is the question that I want you to notice: "Adam, where art thou?" Now that is a significant question and there is a significant answer. The statement goes to verse 9 for the answer: "I was afraid because I was naked and I hid myself." The fact of the matter was, Adam was in sin; he was tempted and fell because of that sin, and fell away from the advantages that he had possessed up to that time, being with God. He had fallen away from the grace of God and separated himself from the One in whose Presence he had previously walked. The important thing about it is that God was not asking it for information. He knew where Adam was all the time, but He was asking in order to present this man with the evidence of his guilt; that now the man recognizes the fact that he is in sin, that he has violated the only law that God gave him and is in sin. So God asked him: "Adam, where art thou?"

I want to tell you, friends, I believe that God will propound that question to some men in the judgment. Not because He wants to know where they are, but in the sense that everything will be brought into judgment, whether it be good or whether it be evil. God is going to have that question presented, and whether spoken directly to you, the implication is there just the same: "Where are you in relationship to your Father?" Now if you settle that problem, and answer that question effectively, properly, scripturally while you live upon this earth, then the approach of death and the judgment will be of no special concern to you. You will have already answered the question; you will have already made ready yourself with regard to where you are and where you stand in relationship to God. That is the important part of it. I want you to see that where you stand in relationship unto God is the thing that is going to settle your eternal destiny. God is long-suffering to usward, not willing that any should perish, but that all should come to repentance, but when men separate themselves from God and stay away from Him, there is only one thing that can come as a result of the mercy and wisdom and justice of God and that is to banish that one, who is separated from Him, from the presence of Himself into the place prepared for the devil and his angels. I am suggesting that as a place to start tonight. I want you to see, first of all, that God is expecting you to do something about your position relative to Him. He is right where He has always been. The idea of men getting down on their knees and begging God to be reconciled unto man! Reconciliation was the work of the Lord Jesus Christ. Jesus Christ came to this earth as an evidence of God's love and anxiety for man. God sent His Son into the world that the world might be saved by him —"For God so loved the world that he GAVE his only Begotten Son, that whosoever believeth in him should not perish, but have everlasting life." I don't have to ask God to be reconciled to me. The very sending of Jesus is the evidence of His willingness to receive the sinner. For people to beg God to be reconciled is altogether out of keeping with the teaching of the Bible. The point is that man has separated himself from God and man must do the coming back to God. God is right where He has always been, just as He was in the garden of Eden. It wasn't God that left Adam, it was Adam and Eve that left God. People leave God in the sense that they are not willing to accept His will, do His bidding, follow His teaching and become citizens of His kingdom.

Sometimes members of the church leave the church even after they have followed the Lord for a time. You need to think in regard to "where art thou?" Now, I am interested in Old Testament examples, but I want you to notice a statement that is made in the New Testament. Actually these things which were written aforetime were written for our admonition and learning, as an example to us. That is the teaching of the apostle Paul, that these things which we have in the Old Testament were written for our admonition, and so I am admonishing us tonight that we think about the relative position that we occupy with respect to God.

But there is another one in the fourth chapter and the 9th verse where we have the question that God propounded to Cain. He said to Cain: "Where is Abel, thy brother?" Genesis 4:9. Cain lied when he said, "I know not." Then he asked, "Am I my brother's keeper?" That is an important question. You remember the story about how Cain slew his brother, Abel. Abel's sacrifice was made by faith—the Bible says so in Hebrews 11: "By faith Abel offered unto God a more excellent sacrifice than Cain." How did he offer it? By faith. Well, did Cain offer his by faith? The Bible tells us that Abel did, and it was more escellent than was Cain's, so there must have been some difference between them. I think I can thus reason from the passage of scripture that says, "Faith cometh by hearing, and hearing by the word of God." So God must have instructed Cain and Abel in regard to how the sacrifice must be offered. The Bible doesn't give specific instructions about that, but the question I want you to see is that after Cain and Abel offered their sacrifices, Cain was wroth—he was mad—because God didn't have respect to his sacrifice and he did have respect unto Abel's sacrifice because it was offered by faith. Now then, "Where is Abel thy brother?" Cain said, "I don't know," and then asked God the question, "Am I my brother's keeper?" I want you to think about that for just a few minutes as I briefly review some of these facts for you to think about.

Here was a man who was actually asking God whether or not that he was his brother's keeper after God had asked him the question, "Where is Abel, thy brother?"

You need to recognize both of those questions. Number one: "Where is Abel, thy brother?" My point with regard to the application of it is this: Are we concerned, or should we be concerned, about our brethren in the Lord? We most certainly should. That is not only the business of the elders of the church, it is the duty of every child of God to be concerned about his brother in Christ. "Where is Abel thy brother?" Where is my Christian brother? Where does he stand in relationship to God all right, but not only that, where is he? That is the point that was propounded to Cain. Where is he NOW? Now God did not say to Adam, "Where art thou now?" He knew Adam was in the garden hiding among the trees, but He asked Cain the question, "I want to know where is thy brother because there is no evidence of his being about." Then God said, "Listen, Cain, Thy brother's blood crieth unto me from the ground." Friends, I think we ought to be concerned about our brethren in Christ.

I remember a few years ago, preaching at a congregation that had maybe a hundred and fifty members, and several elders and several deacons who were active in the Lord's work. I had been preaching there for two or three years at that time and I had become so accustomed to the members of the church, or the people, as they sat in their respective places that I could look over the audience for a few minutes and then go back in my study, take a list of the membership and check off every name that was absent from that group. I think I could almost do that within a period of a few weeks, if I could get sufficiently well acquainted with them to tie the face and name together, and certainly one could do it if he lived there for several years. Well, as I was preaching that Sunday morning I remember I noted and made mental calculation of the fact that there were, as I recall, 22 members of the church who were the relatives of the elders and the deacons missing from their places that Sunday morning. It had been happening a few times, you know; there would be quite a number of them absent, but there were about 22 who were absent relatives of the elders and deacons, the officers of the church. You know, sometimes a preacher just gets filled to the point that he has got to blow off a little steam. Sometimes he gets so fretted that he must blow off a little steam and that was my situation. I announced to the congregation when the sermon was over that I would like to have a business meeting with the elders and deacons down stairs where we usually had our business meeting. Well, after the meeting was over they nonchalantly walked down, not knowing what the preacher had in mind. They were sitting around there, and of course their unconcerned attitude just added fuel to the fire. I was very much concerned about something that apparently they were not concerned about. I started off my speech with these words: "Do you know where your kinfolks are today?" And they straightened up and said: "Well, no, we don't know." I said, "Where is so and so, and so and so, and so and so, and I named the daughters and the sons of the elders and the deacons, and the mothers and fathers of some of them who were pillars in the church—and I guess maybe you could spell that p-i-l-l-o-w in applying it to some. Anyhow they were members of the church and were supposed to be loyal and strong in the kingdom of God, relatives, close relatives— brothers and sisters—of some of them. I asked them, "I wonder where they are today?" I said, "I want you men to know this: I worry myself sick about the members of this church, and apparently, so far as I can see, some of you are not concerned about your own kinfolks. Now I want to know if this question applies to you: "Where is Abel thy brother?" I said that to them as I remember, at least I used words to that effect.

Now, I am saying that to you tonight, brother, "Where is Abel thy brother?" Are you concerned about the members of the church as you ought to be? And I am not talking to the elders of the church tonight as I was that Sunday morning I just mentioned. I just said that, about that example, to show you that not only should they have been concerned, but every member of the church ought to be concerned, not only about their kinfolks but about all their brethren in the Lord.

I have wondered a few times in my life—who is the one that is supposed to get the grayest hair from worrying over indifferent members of the church? Did you ever think about that? Some people seem to think it is supposed to be the preacher or the elders. I remember a fellow who said one time to me, I don't remember the exact language he used, but it was along this line: "Oh, the elders are supposed to feed the flock." Well, you know, that is right. But I will tell you something else that perhaps you had not thought about: the flock ought to be interested enough to recognize their own responsibility to "get up to the trough." I think they have an obligation too. I preach on the qualifications and responsibilities of the elders and that is right; but I also preach on the qualifications and responsibilities of the members. Some members of the church seem to have the idea, "now you elders come and get me if you want me to come; you are supposed to feed me." You know this: The elders are not supposed to run you down and cram it down your throat. They are supposed to oversee every kind of teaching, every kind of preaching that is done in the pulpit or in the class room and privately in the homes. That is right.

Brother, my point tonight is this: "Where is Abel thy brother?" Whose responsibility is he? Well, it is your responsibility, it is mine as a member of the body of Christ. It is the duty of the elders as the bishops of the flock. Do you know, the word that we translate "bishop, elder, overseer or pastor of the flock" also has the meaning of "superintendent?" The elders are "superintendents" of the flock; that is the idea conveyed in the thought of overlooking the flock. But we individually are the keepers of our brethren. You think about that! God may ask you that question. I have known members of the church, women whose husbands were not members of the church, who reminded me of a butterfly flitting about from flower to flower, interested in everything under heaven except their own husbands. They expect the preacher and the elders and everybody else to do everything in their power to convert him to Christ, while they are not doing one single solitary thing to convert that husband to the truth of Christ. I have known husbands whose wives were not Christians, and they would take an indifferent and sometimes a belligerent attitude with respect to whether they had any responsibility in the matter or not. Listen, friends, I think it is an obligation that all of us have. You have an obligation to every individual that may be in the church, or out of it for that matter. Your relationship to that individual means that you have a responsibility, an obligation, that is directly dependent upon you for its performance.

But I want us to notice still another in the same book of Genesis, found in chapter 32, beginning with verse 28. You will remember the story of Jacob wrestling with an angel. That is an unusual and unique situation, I grant you, but it likewise teaches a great truth. As they were wrestling and Jacob was about to overcome the angel, (you remember the angel touched the hollow of his thigh and he limped all the rest of his days) he asked a question of Jacob and here is the question: "Jacob, what is thy name?" Jacob answered that his name was Jacob, and the angel replied, "Thy name shall be called no more Jacob, but Israel." Do you know what that means, friends? That is a significant thing. Israel! Israel! Look at it (writes name on board). When you call the name of God's people under the Old Covenant, when you refer to them as descendants of Jacob, you call them Israelites. That simply meant that when he changed the name from Jacob to Israel, it was far, far more significant than the name Jacob. But when he asked him, "What is thy name?" he said, "My name is Jacob." Well, he said:

"I am going to give you another name." And he gave him another name—"Thy name shall no more be called Jacob, but you are going to be known by the name, Israel."

Now look: the word EL is the "God part" of Jacob's new name, Isra-EL. Where you see the letters E L on the end of a Hebrew word, that indicates something in connection with God. Israel! When you call the name of the Israelites, you call the name of God under the Old Covenant. When you call the name of God's people today, you call the name of Christ: CHRIST-IAN. That is what my name is! You ought to be a CHRISTIAN, and appreciate the significance of it. "What is thy name?" Well, somebody says, Is that important? I think it is; I think it is important. I will tell you why. I think it is important to individuals. Sometimes people will say, "Oh, I wouldn't say there is anything in a name." Here is a religious body that wears this denominational name, and here is another religious body that wears another denominational name, and some say, "Oh, they are just the names that people wear; they don't have any significance." Why, friends, we all know better than that. Everybody knows that names have a significance. I have the strangest name you ever heard of in your life—P-I-C-K-U-P, Pickup. Isn't that a silly name? But it is the name my Daddy gave me; it is the family name and I still wear it. I have had lots of trouble with it. I never can make people know what it is and yet it is as simple as A, B, C. It means something to me. Now I have actually gotten into a little trouble once in a while about it. Just like everybody else, I get irritated once in a while about things. I am usually very genial and easy to get along with, but you can keep sticking a fellow, and just keep sticking him until by and by it will irritate him a little bit. I have had those things happen to me with regard to my name several times. I never will forget when I graduated from grammar school. We had a Jew who lived in the city where I was living who was called out to present the diplomas. Now I don't know how many of you younger people who are here tonight, (or maybe some of the elder ones) who went through that thrill. I don't think we give diplomas at the 8th grade now, do we? But they used to do it. Oh, I remember how I swelled with pride on that occasion, when I realized that I was about to receive my diploma. This Jew got up before the crowd and saw that here was a chance to make a joke out of something and he made some funny remarks about my name, and it just took all the joy out of my receiving my diploma on that occasion. I lost a couple of years in those few seconds it took me to walk down the aisle with my face flaming red (I am sure) while he made some funny remarks about my name. I wasn't responsible for the name that my father had given me. However, all that is important, only in its application. When you call the name of God's child today you call the name of the Lord Jesus Christ. Don't you ever go around and say, "There is nothing in a name." That would never do. You really don't mean that. Suppose you were to make a statement like that—"There is nothing in a name?" All right. Jesus Christ is a name, therefore, there is nothing in Jesus Christ! You wouldn't say that. You know the only time people make such a statement as: "There is nothing in a name?" It is when they do not have anything else to say and they can't answer the argument, and so they just say: "Oh, there is nothing in a name."

I want to read something to you and let you see whether or not there is anything in a name. I remember a few years ago there was a Baptist man, a fellow in whom I was interested, a member of the Baptist church who claimed that he was a "Baptist-Christian." Well, I said, "I am just a Christian. You say you are a Baptist-Christian?"

"Yes sir, I am a Baptist-Christian; I am proud of the fact that I am a Baptist."

Well I said, "I am proud of the fact that I am just a Christian, and I want to read something."

"Well," he said, "it doesn't make any difference about the name; I am a Christian too."

I said, "You don't know whether it makes any difference or not."

"No," he said, "it doesn't make any special difference."

I said, "I want to tell you, brother, you may have to answer that question at the last day"—and I was thinking about this sermon you know—"you may have to answer that question about the name."

He said, "Oh, I don't know that I will have to answer that question in the judgment."

All right, let us see if we can find out. In the 4th chapter of the Book of Acts of Apostles, beginning at verse 8, "Then Peter, filled with the Holy Ghost, said unto them, Ye rulers of the people, and elders of Israel, if we this day be examined of the good deed done to the impotent man, by what means he is made whole; be it known unto you all, and to all the people of Israel, that by the name of Jesus Christ of Nazareth, whom ye crucified, whom God raised from the dead, even by him doth this man stand here before you whole. This is the stone which was set at nought of you builders, which is become the head of the corner. Neither is there salvation in any other: for there is none other name under heaven given among men, whereby we must be saved."

Now do you suppose that is going to be significant at the last day? Let me read you one other passage of scripture. In the 20th chapter of the Book of Revelation and the 13th verse: "And the sea gave up the dead which were in it; and death and hell delivered up the dead which were in them: and they were judged every man according to their works." Are you going to have something tacked on to you in the judgment that you can't read about in the Bible? Are you going to be wearing some denominational name when you come before God in the great day? You ask a fellow what he is religiously and see if he doesn't mention his denominational name, nine times out of ten, before he even refers to the name "Christian." In discussion people quote it the other way, but that is not the way that it is done in actual practice. The Bible says that you are going to have to give an account for the things that you have done. One of those things is the name you wear. I don't want anything in the judgment that I will have to be offering excuses for, and when God asks me about my name, I want to say to Him: "Lord, I wore the name of the Lord Jesus Christ; I was not a hyphenated Christian of any kind. I was simply a Christian. I was a saint of the Lord. I was a child of God. I was a member of the body of Christ, but my name was "Christian.'" I want that to stand out in my life. I am not concerned about being anything else. I am not a member of anything else under heaven except the church built by Jesus Christ.

I have always been embarrassed to have something around me I had to make excuses for. I have had to do that a few times. Nearly all of us have something that we have had to apologize for. I remember back in my courting days I had a little old "Model T Ford" automobile that was cut down to make a "skeeter." You know what a "skeeter" is? I know some of you older folk do. It was a Model T automobile with the top taken off, the body taken off, and one of these little "racer" bodies put on it. We called them "skeeters." It was an old 1917 model but it meant a lot to me. Most cars back then would sometimes give trouble. My "Model T" gave me trouble nearly all the time. I would get in the thing and start to take my girl for a ride. She would get up in the seat and get all settled and I would turn on the switch, you know; they had a long switch-key about that long (measures on hands about four inches) and you turned it over on the side and go round in front of the thing and calmly pull up on the crank. I would turn on the key and then stand back and take my time—she would be waiting—and I would pull out this little thing over here (the choke) and let it suck in some gas, and pull the crank up again, and nothing

would happen. I would do that three or four times. Then
I would begin the process of spinning the motor with the
crank. I would "jigger" this and "jigger" that, and
"jigger" the other, and touch this and touch that, and
then I would go around to her and say: "Honey, it is going
to start in just a minute; we will get going soon now."
She would just sit up there, you know; everything all
right. By and by it would begin to chug away, after I
had made one apology after another for the fact that it
would not start, all of which embarrassed me no end.
Friends, I don't want to have something hung onto me
when I get up yonder that I have to apologize for; I don't
want anything about me that I am going to have to offer
an excuse for and have to say: "Lord, I know I brought
this thing along because it seemed all right down there,
although I know you didn't authorize it."

Take the matter of the kind of worship. I love the
sound of mechanical instrumental music. I would have
one in the church building if it were left to me. I love
the sound of a sweet pipe organ myself. I don't know
about Phillips over here, but, brother, I love the sound of
a sweet pipe organ. I just don't see anything in the
world wrong with it myself. I think that instrumental
music is just as beautiful and sweet as can be, and if it
were left to me, brother, I would settle that thing: I
would have one. But you know, friends, there is one
good reason why I couldn't have a mechanical instrument
in the worship of the Lord. Why? Not because I don't
like it. Well why? Because I would have to do some
strong apologizing to the Lord when I come before Him
in the judgment. Now I said the foregoing to make you
see that there is no prejudice on my part. I am not
prejudiced against instrumental music. Some people think
that people of the churches of Christ are just mean, or
they don't like music! Brother, I do; I like music myself.
"Well, why don't you have it in the church? Why don't
you have it in the worship?" Here is my reason: God
doesn't authorize it, and when we get up yonder I don't

want the Lord asking me: "What about mechanical instruments you used down there at Howard Avenue church of Christ in Tampa?" I would have to say: "Lord, you know how sweet the music sounds to the people. I know you didn't authorize it, but it sounded mighty good to us."

Brother, you can read this Book from beginning to end and the man doesn't live who can find one single, solitary passage of scripture from the beginning of the New Testament to the close of it which authorizes the use of mechanical instrumental music in worship to God under the Christian dispensation. There isn't any authority for it, and when I get before the Lord I don't want Him to say to me, "What about that thing?"

Let me read you a passage over here with regard to the matter of going beyond the command of the Lord. In I Samuel 15th chapter and the 3rd verse, when Saul was about to go down among the Amalekites, God told him to go down and utterly destroy them from the face of the earth. Later, when he came back, there was the bleating of the sheep and the lowing of the oxen, all of which should have been killed down there in that country of the Amelekites. When Saul insisted he had obeyed God's instructions, Samuel went out and asked Saul a question. Here is the question: "What meaneth then this bleating of the sheep and the lowing of the oxen that I hear in my ears?" God had said, "Go and smite the Amelekites and utterly destroy all that they have, and spare them not, but slay both man and woman and infant and suckling and ox and sheep and camel and ass." That included all. But Saul, instead of slaying them, listened to what the people had to say and they decided that they would bring some of them back. When Saul got back and reported that he had done the bidding of the Lord God, Samuel said: "If you have done the bidding of the Lord, what meaneth then the lowing of the oxen and the bleating of these sheep that I hear in mine ears. What does that mean if you have done the Lord's will? What means this?"

I think I can apply that to instrumental music in the worship. I will tell you how. God said: "Singing, and making melody in your hearts unto God." "Singing with grace in your hearts unto the Lord." "In the midst of the congregation will I sing praise unto God." "Is any among you merry, let him sing psalms." Back in Matthew and Mark we have the two references to the statement that when they "had sung an hymn, they went out into the mount of Olives." Of the nine passages that we find in the New Testament, everyone of them refers to the kind of music that God wants us to make. When we come before Him in that day and say: "Lord, we have done the bidding of our Lord in worship." God may ask: "What was that sound that I used to hear coming from the Clearwater church when you put in that mechanical instrument without any authority from me?" You want to think about this thing, friends, for there is a principle involved here, and the principle is that you need to settle the question with regard to "what meaneth these things?" Or "What are these things that you are doing that you have no authority for in the word of the living God?"

Well, I pass on to another one, and I am looking at a scripture in II Kings the 5th chapter and 25th verse. It is the story of Elisha and his little servant boy, Gehazi. Did you ever hear that one? Friends, I know you have read that, and I'm sure you know the story, but I am going to briefly review it for you. You remember that Naaman the leper came by, and as the story is told here in II Kings 5, he had leprosy and wanted to be cured from that leprosy. He finally got the instructions to go to the prophet—he had gone first to the king and finally came to the prophet of God—and the prophet sent his servant boy out and said: "You go tell him to dip in the river Jordan seven times." Naaman was worth. He didn't want to do that but finally at the persuasion of his own servant boy, he did go and dip seven times in the Jordan, and lo, behold his flesh was as white and clean as the flesh of a little child. He was happy over the whole thing. He rushed back to the prophet of God and said, "I want to give you something." But, of course, the prophet said, "There is no charge for anything, please sir; you just go on your way." Finally, after some exchange of conversation, he journeyed toward his Syrian home. But there was a little servant boy, Gehazi, standing by, and he heard this man offer his master some changes of garments and some silver, and his heart was covetous. When Elisha went back in the room, he followed Naaman and caught up with him down the road and told him a story. He said: "Naaman, there were two young men who have come in since you were there, and my master has sent me to ask you if you will renew that offer of giving us something for these sons of the prophets." Naaman was tickled to death, and he said: "All right, I'll be glad to." So he burdened him with the gifts that he gave him. Gehazi took them and put them in his house. I can almost see him as he brushes off his hands, a job well done. Then he looked up and Elisha stood in the door. Now listen and let me read it for you. Elisha said to Gehazi: "Gehazi, whence comest thou?" And Gehazi gives a rather unusual answer. He said: "Thy servant went no whither." Now here is what that really means: Elisha simply said, "Gehazi, where have you been?" And Gehazi said, 'I ain't been no where." But Elisha said, "Yes you have." He said: "Didn't my heart go with you? Didn't I know what you were doing? The leprosy of Naaman shall cleave unto thee, and unto thy seed forever." And he went out from his presence a leper as white as snow.

Listen, friends, that is important! Where have you been all of these years? That is my application of it. What have you been doing? Where have YOU been? Well, some people have been wasting their time, wasting their opportunities, wasting themselves in the cause of Satan. God is not pleased with that, friends. You need to recognize your responsibility and obligation before God, and day after day do your very best to achieve a greater success in His kingdom because God may ask you in the judgment: "Where have you been, and what have you been doing?" You know, Gehazi didn't know that through the power that his master had that he could know where he was. He had an idea that he was getting away with something, but you know, friends, you never do with God. You NEVER do with God! Your husband may not know what you are doing; your wife may not know what you are doing; your children may not understand where you have been, or what has been the burden of your activity, but I want to tell you this: God knows all about you. He understands the very thinking of your mind, and He knows where you are, and not only where you are but what you have been doing all of this time. That is a serious thing. Here I am. I have lived for a long while in this old world. I have had many opportunities. Have I accepted them? Or have I wasted some of my time? I lose some sleep over that question, friends. I don't know whether I am doing all that I am capable of doing or not. I don't know whether or not that I have been carrying my share of the load. Am I using my time, my talent, my money in the service of God to the greatest advantage. Brother Akin, one of the greatest men, perhaps, that you will find anywhere among those who are extremely wealthy, once made a remark somewhat like this: "I am concerned, not so much now about the ordinary things that used to bother me or trouble me as I went along the way, but I am concerned with whether or not I am using my money in the service of God as I should be doing." Brother, that is important! Are you using yourself and all that you are in His service as He wants you to use yourself in His service? That is important! My point is: Where have you been? Have you been serving the devil most of your time? Then you ought to, with renewed enthusiasm, enter into the work of the Lord and say, "I want to redeem the time." Paul uses that expression: "redeeming the time, for the days are evil." Oh, my friends, they are; they are very evil. We don't have very many years to get the job done. Have we been using ourselves? Where have we been? What are we doing in the service of our God?

Finally, tonight I want you to see one example from the New Testament. Do you remember the trial of Jesus before Pontius Pilate? The Bible says that prior to that occasion when he was tried before Pontius, he was taken by a mob, and among other things it is stated that Simon Peter was so enthusiastic about this whole thing, when that mob came up to take his Lord, he reached over and got the sword out of the scabbard that was near by, slung it at the fellow who was nearest to him to cut off his head. The fellow ducked his head just in time and it cut off his ear. Peter wasn't hitting at that fellow's ear, he was hitting at his head. He was intending to chop his head off, but he just turned it in time, evidently, and the sword cut off the ear. The Lord healed it. But that shows the enthusiasm of Peter. The Lord said: "Put up your sword; they that take the sword shall perish by the sword." Then, finally, as the mob took him, the disciples dropped away one by one, and even enthusiastic Peter, the Bible says, "Followed from afar off." But by and by they got into the court yard, and as they were standing around and Peter was warming himself over by the fire that was built up by the men who were the enemies of the Lord. He wasn't in a friendly place. These people were the Lord's enemies, but he was standing there warming himself and somebody came up and asked him the question that I want you to notice now. Here it is: "Peter, are you a disciple of Jesus?" That is the substance of the question. "Peter, are you a disciple?" He said: "NO," Then later the question came again, the second, and even the third time. The third time, the Bible says, Peter cursed and swore and said, No! I am not a disciple!" And when he did the Lord turned and looked at him. Then, we learn, Peter went out and wept bitterly, for he had heard the cock crow and he had already denied the Lord three times, just as the Lord had predicted that he would.

Listen, friends, here is my question: "Are you a Christian, not according to the standards of men, but according to the standards of this Book?" Are you a Christian? You know sometimes people will almost apologize when somebody refers to them as a Christian. Why you have heard them and so have I. Somebody will say: "Are you a Christian?" And that person says: "Well, I guess so." Don't you know whether you are a member of the body of Christ? Don't you know whether you have believed in him with all your heart, and turned away from sin and error, and have confessed him before men and have been buried with him in baptism for the remission of your sins? Don't you know??? You ought to know. When somebody asks you if you are a Christian, and you can turn to that Bible and read what God says is the plan of salvation for putting you into the church and making you a Christian, you are all right. When somebody asks you that question, say: "Thank God, YES!" Be sufficiently emphatic about it to let people know where you stand. Instead of being weak and wishy-washy about it, say: "Thank God, YES!" You ought to be proud of it, proud to wear the name of the Lord. Well, Peter went out after that and wept bitterly.

But you know, friends, there came another day in Peter's life, and it is my last question tonight. It happened after the Lord was put to death. I don't know where Peter was during that time, but I know he was somewhere. He must have known all about it, and he may have even seen his Lord, possibly did, as he was writhing in pain upon the cross dying for the sins of the world. Peter became very sad. I know that. All of the apostles and disciples were sad. We know that too. Finally the Lord was taken down from that cross and put in the tomb of Joseph of Arimathaea, and on the third day he came forth victorious over death, hades and the grave and appeared unto his disciples. I am not going to review all of them, but one of the appearances was when these men were down on the sea fishing, fishing on the little sea of

Galilee, where they had been many times. Peter had said, "I am going fishing," and the others said, "we will go with you," and there they were out there fishing when the Lord appeared on the shore and spoke to them. He said: "Cast your net down over here on the other side." And they did and when they pulled it up it was full of fish. John said, "Peter, it is the Lord." Peter swam to shore and the others came in the boat. Jesus had a fire going with fish and bread prepared, so they had breakfast together that morning. After the breakfast was over, the Lord talked to Peter. He said: "Peter, lovest thou me more than these?" Peter said: "Yes, Lord, I love you." Then the Lord asked him the question the second time: "Peter, lovest thou me more than these?" And Peter replied the second time and said: "Yes, Lord, I love you." And then the third time he asked the question: "Peter, lovest thou me more than these?" Peter said: "Lord, you know everything, you know I love you."

Now I wonder why he asked him the question three times? Some people will say it was because he denied him three times. I don't think that is the answer. That may have had something to do with it, but I seriously doubt it and I am going to tell you why. There are two words in the Greek vocabulary that we translate "love." One of them is *love on a high plain*, or love of the reason. This word is *agapao*. The other word denotes a *love down here on a human or brotherly plain*, the love of the feelings or affections. This second word is *phileo*. The first time the Lord spoke to Peter on that occasion, he said, "Peter, *agapao?*" up here; and Peter said: *"Phileo,"* down here. Maybe Peter had learned his lesson, I don't know, but that is the way it was. The second time the Lord said: "Peter, *agapao*"—love way up here; but Peter said: *"Phileo"*—way down here. Then the third time the Lord came down from *agapao;* he came down to *phileo,* for he said: "Peter, *phileo,"* and Peter said: *"Phileo."* What does all this mean? I'll tell you, friends. Peter had boasted prior to that time when he said: "Lord, if every last one of these turn away from you, I will not." The Lord said, "Now look out there, Peter, look out there." Yes, once Peter had boasted of his love for Jesus, but not that morning on the sea of Galilee.

Now I want to tell you why I introduced that as my final question: God wants to know if you love Him! He will not wait until the judgment day to ask you that. He wants to know if you love Him. DO-YOU-LOVE-HIM?? Do you know HOW to show your love for Him? You show your love for Him by obeying the gospel, if you are not a Christian. If you are not a member of the church you can read about in the New Testament, then you demonstrate your love by obeying the gospel. If you are a Christian, you demonstrate it by living the Christian life. Do you love me? is the statement made by the Lord to Peter, and I'm asking you that question tonight. Do you love Him?

A few years ago I was in a meeting at the Moreland Avenue church in Atlanta, Ga. I stayed in a home of a family in which the husband was sick and the mother had to go out and help bring in a part of the family income. There were several children, one of them a little boy by the name of David, about four years old. He was one of the sweetest little fellows I ever saw, but one of the most meddlesome children that God ever made. He liked to meddle with every thing in general and my things in particular, and so he did. He occupied himself every day I was there, or almost every day, meddling with some of the things I had. I could be studying my Bible, getting my sermon ready, and David would come around and get in the way. His mother said to me one day: "Brother Pickup, I know David bothers you some, you are with him a lot alone." There was a maid that came in and sorta looked after the children, a colored girl, but she did not always know where the children were, and she very seldom knew where David was unless I happened to be in the house. The mother said: "Now I understand, Brother Pickup, that you are alone a great deal together, and if David bothers you too much you just paddle him a little bit." Well, I took her at her word. The very next time, which was the very next day, I was trying my very best to get ready for a morning service, or maybe it was an evening service, and David was just as meddlesome as could be and I just stood all I could. I just took the little fellow up, laid my hand on the proper place on his anatomy to get the desired results, and set him down. He ran over in the corner just sobbing and crying like his little heart would break. Well, I was not going to be broken down by his tears, so I put my Bible up before my face and began sternly to study and read as hard as I could, and paid no attention to the crying of the little fellow. It wasn't long, however, until I heard some footsteps coming over to my chair, and as I sat there I felt a little tug as his hand pulled on my sleeve. I looked down sternly in his face, and he looked up at me with his big brown eyes, brimming full of tears, and he said: "Bruvver Pickup, do you lost me?" Of course I did, and that was that. The lesson was over.

Friends, God wants to know that about you. God wants to know if you love Him. A little child can tug on our heart strings and pull mighty hard, but God wants to know if His little child—you are a little child of God— God wants to know if His little child loves Him. The only way that you can prove it is by doing His will. Do you love Him? Then if you do, if you need to do something about your condition, why don't you do it tonight? Why wont you come to the Lord; why wont you come back, backsliding Christians, and confess your faults one to another, and pray one for another? Why don't you make everything right by showing God that you love Him? Will you come tonight while we stand and sing?

OLD FASHION RELIGION

I want to join Brother Phillips in expressing to you my genuine appreciation for your presence, and say that we covet your interest in this lesson tonight as at all other times. We are anxious to do the things that will please the Lord and to present His will in its fullness in such a way that men will understand it, and be moved to either live better or, if out of Christ, to obey the gospel. That is the reason for this meeting, my friends, to present the truth, and to present it plainly but simply and as forcefully as we can to try and persuade men to accept it. I have no other purpose in life than to urge people to be Christians, and to try to teach all who are members of the church to live better, and go to heaven when life is over. I am concerned about such matters and to this end I am preaching the gospel of the Lord Jesus Christ, I trust, in a way that will be acceptable to Him and may be profitable to all who come from time to time.

It has been announced that the sermon tonight is referred to by its title: *Old Fashion Religion*. I think that is a scriptural expression for I believe that these truths we hope to present regarding *Old Fashion Religion* are found in the scriptures. If they are, then the idea is a scriptural teaching or a scriptural idea. I want to call your attention, first of all, to the fact that people in this day, and for a long time, have been thinking in terms of old things. You can hardly go up and down the street but that you pass places of business founded upon the idea that people will buy old things. Old furniture, old relics of different kinds, types and sizes which simply mean that they are thinking in terms of the past. Now I believe we ought to think in terms of the future and the present, but I rather agree that it is profitable to think in terms of the past, and especially so with regard to religion. That is the reason that I endorse such an idea as is expressed in the term "Old Fashion Religion." I rather think to some extent, however, that in material matters we are affected by the psychology of extremes sometimes, which simply means that we are on one end of the line and the old things are on the other end of the line. We want to go back and pick up some of the old things that we have known before. I know it has been interesting to me to observe that many elderly people think in terms of going back to the scenes of their childhood. They think: "I should like to go back to the old swimming hole." Or they say: "I should like to go back and fish where I used to fish." But when they get there the things are not the same. Of course they forget that matters have changed with regard to those things that they left behind as well as they themselves have changed. So while it is important in some matters to think of old things, it is not so important in those as it is in the matters of religion. Many of the old songs are coming back once again. Some of them are becoming quite popular. I personally think that most of them are prettier than some of these "honky-tonk" type of songs you hear today. I like the melody of the old songs. Nearly everybody else does, but it seems that many of the song writers have lost their heads completely and are catering more to the idea of "Jazz"—even in songs— that men like this type that are supposed to be serious.

I really brought up the subject of old songs in order to introduce the next thought. I was preaching over the radio in North Carolina a few years ago this same sermon I am preaching tonight. Sometimes when I am preaching I introduce points that I had not previously thought about using, so as I was pointing out that even some of the so called "old" songs miss the point in some parts, I just broke down on a stanza of "Give Me That Old Time Religion" (here singing). Well, the announcer, who was sitting asleep in the control room just across the way, knew that I had never sung on the radio, and when he heard that singing he aroused up immediately and began to frantically twist the dials of his control panel in front of him for he thought surely he had tuned in on something that ought not to be on the air. There was such a song one time, you remember, that said: "Give Me That Old Time Religion." Don't get uneasy, folks, I am not going to lead it and try to get you to sing it, but I wonder if you remember any of the stanzas of it. I don't have it written down anywhere and I don't know all the stanzas, but I do remember some things they state. For example, one statement says: "It was good for Dad and Mother, it was good for Dad and Mother, so it is good enough for me." Now, friends, do you want a religion of the "Gay Nineties?" The fact that it was good enough for Dad and Mother may not necessarily mean anything after all. "It was good for brother and sister" is another one of the verses. Well, now does that give any special dignity to "Old Fashion Religion?" Are people simply what they are because of what their mothers and fathers and their brothers and sisters are in religion? Many times this is probably true. Many people are members of some denomination, or they are politically what they are, merely because their mothers and fathers or their brothers and sisters or their aunts and uncles were that either religiously or politically. There is another verse that says: "It was good for Paul and Silas." Ah! I'm willing to go back there all right! "It was good for Paul and Silas." Now that gets us right back to the time; that is where I am going to drive down the stake tonight, right back to the days of Paul and Silas. That, my brother, is the old fashion religion that I am talking about tonight. Not the religion that had its beginning in the "Gay Nineties"; not the religion that started some time ago during the "heyday" of some saw-dust trail evangelist, so-called, who went out and stirred up a lot of people and started a new philosophy of religion and referred to that as "Old Time Religion," when it was modern to the "nth" degree in all its implications. Friends, I am talking tonight about the religion of the New Testament. I want to speak to you then on "Old Fashion Religion" based upon that.

First of all I want to call your attention to a statement that is made in the 12th chapter of Romans in which the writer says: "I beseech you therefore, brethren, by the mercies of God, that ye present your bodies a living sacrifice, holy, acceptable unto God, which is your reasonable service." Then he goes on to say, "And be not conformed to this world: but be ye transformed by the renewing of your mind, that ye may prove what is that good, and acceptable, and perfect, will of God." Don't be conformed to this world, but be transformed by the renewing of your mind, that ye may prove what is that good, and acceptable, and perfect, will of God. Now the point I want you to get in that passage of scripture is that, "Be not fashioned according to this world" is an expression that Paul uses in writing to the church in Rome, which means we are not to be fashioned according to some modern innovation, not a fashioning according to some modern idea that is as far away from the New Testament as the east is from the west. Paul is preaching conformity to God's will, that we are not to be fashioned according to the teachings of the world but according to the teaching of the Lord Jesus Christ and the apostles. My friends, I believe, therefore, that I could say negatively tonight that the Old Fashion Religion is not a religion that is fashioned according to the world, but a religion fashioned according to the teaching of the New Testament. That is a simple statement, and it is fraught with no particular ideals of mine or any other man, but it contains the ideals of God that are based upon a "thus saith the Lord." That is the thing that is important, so we can say negatively that Old Fashion Religion is not a religion that is fashioned according to the teachings of the world, or by the way of the world, but it is built upon the ideals and ideas of God. Well, it may not necessarily be a religion that satisfies the councils of men. It is not based upon that. Neither is it based or fashioned ACCORDING to the world, neither fashioned ACCORDING to the councils of men. Although men may be intelligent, although men may have much learning, the religion of the New Testament does not depend upon such.

A few years ago I sat one day as a visitor in a class room in a theological seminary which is operated by men who are supposed to know a great deal about the Bible. The name of it, as I recall, was the Virginia Seminary, a school operated by the Episcopal Church in Alexandria, Virginia. In the class rooms of that institution—it is a graduate school—are college men, studying to be Episcopal priests, who listen to the expose of the Bible by men who are supposed to know. I remember an expression used by one of them on one occasion according to Brother Hugo McCord. The professor in his lecture on that particular day referred to the fact that many people use the Bible as authority. Why he said: "Well it is true that we read the Bible and study the Bible, and it is a good Book and all of that, down in the Bible Belt they use the Bible as authority on a par with Shakespeare!" Now, friends, I have told you that to say this: The religion of the New Testament is not the religion that is fashioned after the councils of men! It doesn't matter whether people think that there are sections of the country that they refer to as "The Bible Belt"—that does use the Bible as authority —or whether they disregard such sections as that. I want to tell you that true Christianity, the religion of the word of God which is in force today, does not depend upon what any man, or set of men, may think or teach. Those people who love the Lord, whether they live in the south or the north, across the ocean or where ever they are, know that the religion of the New Testament is predicated upon God's divine will and not upon the authority of men or the councils of men.

With those two negative ideas, let us get to a positive statement that is found in the New Testament. I want to call your attention, first of all tonight, to the fact that Old Fashion Religion is THE RELIGION OF THE OLDEST CHURCH. What do we mean by the oldest church? Well, I want to tell you. I am going to read a passage of scripture that I have read once before, but I want to read it again because I want to emphasize it. It is found in the 16th chapter of the book of Matthew and beginning at verse 13: "When Jesus came into the coasts of Caesarea Philippi, he asked his disciples, saying, Whom do men say that I the Son of man am? And they said, Some say that thou art John the Baptist: some, Elias; and others, Jeremias, or one of the prophets. He saith unto them, But whom say ye that I am? And Simon Peter answered and said, Thou art the Christ, the Son of the living God. And Jesus answered and said unto him, Blessed art thou, Simon Barjona: for flesh and blood hath not revealed it unto thee, but my Father which is in heaven. And I say also unto thee, That thou art Peter, and upon this rock I will build my church; and the gates of hell shall not prevail against it."

Now my first thought tonight is that the religion of the Bible is the religion of the oldest church. What one is it? The Roman Catholics claim that it is the Catholic church. They say that when the Lord made that statement I just read that he was talking about building His church upon Peter. If you have made even a casual study of the Bible, however, you will know better than that. There isn't a person alive today that can successfully defend such an idea as that. The Lord wasn't saying: "I am going to build my church upon you, Peter." The gender of the nouns employed in the original language shows that this is not true. The word *petros*, which is a noun of the masculine gender, referred to Peter, which means a small rock. The noun *petra*, which is a noun of the feminine gender, is one that means a great ledge of rock and refers to the truth that had been confessed by Peter —not to Peter himself. But even if I didn't know anything about that, there are passages of scripture which refer to the Lord Jesus Christ as the "chief corner stone" of the building, and "head of the body," etc. One passage does state that it is built upon the "foundation of the apostles and the prophets." But what of that? The Roman Catholic church is not hinted at in the statement Jesus made or anywhere else in the Bible. Now here is

my thought: Jesus said, "I will build my church." I believe that when the Lord made that statement he was
making a statement relative to the oldest church. I believe you will accept that conclusion too, if you will think
about it for a few minutes. Jesus said, "Upon this rock
I will build MY church"—that is the Lord's church; and
when I call it the "church of Christ," THAT is what I am
talking about. I am not using a denominational expression. I don't refer to the church as a denomination. I
couldn't do so, for in order for me to do that it would have
to mean that the Lord has brought about in his body a
division and divided the church up into various and sundry denominations, and that is not so. The Lord said:
"There is one body, there is one baptism, there is one
faith, there is one Lord, there is one God, there is one
hope"; the seven ones in Ephesians, chapter 4, would
demonstrate that it could never be divided up into these
groups. Listen, friends, what is the religion of the oldest
church? The Lord said, It is my church. Now you think
about that. You have read that many times, but maybe
you have overlooked the significance of the statement.
Does the Lord say, I am building all of the different
churches in the world? Why no! Look! The Bible refers
to it as "THE church" or "THE body of Christ." In I
Corinthians 12:12-27 Paul not only refers to it as "the
body," but he says "there is BUT one body." Sometimes,
you know, people say, "You ought not to say that there is
but one church." Then let me ask: How many did the
Lord build? He built only one. The old fashion religion
I am talking about tonight is the religion of that oldest
church, the church that the Lord built—not man.

When Paul was about to leave the elders at Ephesus,
recorded in the 20th chapter of Acts and the 28th verse,
he spoke to those elders and said: "Feed the church of
God which he hath purchased with his own blood." Well,
do you call it the church of God which he hath purchased
with his own blood." Well, do you call it the church of
God? Why sure I do. That is how Paul refers to it on

several occasions. Now right here to the Ephesians elders
he says: "Feed the church of God," as recorded in the
King James Version. This particular version that I have
in my hand is the American Standard Version, this one
that is on the stand is the King James, here is a Roman
Catholic Version which has the imprimatur of the Pope
on it. It doesn't make any difference which one I read
from because they are all correct in the original and they
all make the same statement: "Upon this rock I will build
my church," says all of them, and when Paul refers to it
he calls it the "church of God," or "the church of the
Lord" which he purchased with his own blood. Now
which one of the members of the Godhead came down
from heaven and was crucified on the cross, and purchased
the church with his own blood? It was the Lord Jesus
Christ; it was the God, Christ, the second member of the
Godhead. There is God the Father, God the Son, God the
Holy Spirit. Now which one of them came down and
died on the cross? It was the Lord Christ. Therefore,
when I speak of it as the "church of the Lord," I am saying the same thing as when I talk about the "church of
God." I am referring to the same institution.

Now do you see these points, friends? I want you to
understand that the Lord teaches that He built His church
which is the oldest church—the one that began on the
day of Pentecost when the Lord's Holy Spirit came down
and filled the apostles, and these apostles began to speak
with other tongues as the Spirit gave them utterance.
The Bible tells us there were dwelling in Jerusalem Jews,
devout men out of every nation under heaven. Peter
preached unto them, they heard the gospel, believed it,
and obeyed it as commanded, and the 47th verse of Acts
2 says the Lord added them to the church. Now my point
is that the old fashion religion I am talking about tonight,
is the religion of the oldest church on earth.

Let us notice another important thing about this old
fashion religion I am talking about: It contains THE
OLDEST LAW OF PARDON. Well, what is that? It is

the law of pardon which is found in the New Testament.
I will begin in the second chapter of Acts and just recite
a few statements from each of several chapters. In Acts
2 Peter is preaching. He says in substance to the people:
"You have crucified and slain the Lord Jesus Christ; you
have disobeyed God, you have turned away from Him."
Finally, when they were convinced of it, they cried out
and said: "Men and brethren, what shall we do?" Then
Peter said unto them: "Repent, and be baptized every
one of you in the name of Jesus Christ for the remission
of sins, and ye shall receive the gift of the Holy Spirit.
For the promise is unto you and your children, and to all
that are afar off, even as many as the Lord our God shall
call. And with many other words did he testify and
exhort, saying, Save yourselves from this untoward generation." The Bible says, "Then they that gladly received his word were baptized: and the same day there
were added unto them about three thousand souls." Thus
we see that these people who had heard the gospel, and
who believed the gospel, OBEYED the gospel and were
added together on that day. Now verse 47 says that the
Lord "added daily to the church such as should be saved."
You see, therefore, that the law of pardon, as it was
executed there on that day, involved the idea of preaching
the gospel of Christ. That is number one. It involved
the idea of the hearing of the gospel of Christ. The Bible
says that you have to hear in order to obey. The next one
shows that they not only heard it, but they believed it.
"They that gladly received his word." That is faith. They
had to believe it or they would not have received it, so
they received the word of the Lord, therefore, they believed the word of the Lord. So we have all of those
things constituting the law of pardon. Well, what are
they? Number one: They had to hear the gospel of the
Lord Jesus Christ; they had to believe the gospel of the
Lord Jesus Christ; then they had to repent of their sins
and finally they had to be baptized for the remission of
sins." When they had done that, the Bible says the Lord

added them to the church. Now, what was that for? That is the oldest law of pardon.

I have had men to say: "Now then, Brother Pickup, I know that goes back, way back, but what about going back to John 3:16?" All right, I had just as soon go there as anywhere else. I believe that likewise represents the law of pardon. "Well, I didn't know you believed that," they say. Let me read it for you. "For God so loved the world, that he gave his only begotten Son, that whosoever believeth in him should not perish, but have everlasting life." "You mean to tell me that you believe that passage states that people who believe will be saved?" YES! "Well I didn't think you preachers who preach in the church of Christ preached that." Well, you just didn't know maybe. You misunderstood it somewhere. "Do you mean, Brother Pickup, you believe salvation is by faith?" Sure, salvation is by faith. "Well, I didn't know you believed that. I thought you believed salvation was some other way." No, friends, salvation is by faith. Do you know where the trouble is? It is when somebody comes along and says it is by "faith only." That is where I buck up my back. Just as long as a fellow will leave that off (pointing to "ONLY "on the blackboard), I will go right along with it. The Bible does say that salvation is by faith, but not by faith only. Faith only would cut out the blood; faith only would cut out the name; faith only would cut out repentance. Nobody believes that salvation is by faith only, I don't care who it is. You say: "Oh, we teach that down at the church where we go." Oh, no you don't. You just think you do. You ask the preacher if they teach salvation by faith only. If they do, ask where repentance cames in. "Oh, repentance is included." All right, it is not by faith only, if repentance is included. No, friends, the trouble is that people want to get away from the law of pardon; they want to cut out one thing and that is baptism. It doesn't make any difference to me about baptism, I had just as soon leave it out so far as I am personally concerned, but the Lord has put it in. The Bible says:

"He that believeth and is baptized shall be saved," therefore, baptism is a condition of salvation, no matter how many times you may read to the contrary in the writings of men. Now watch: This Book says, and Acts 2:38 is my authority, that these people heard the preaching of the Lord Jesus Christ and accepted what they had heard. They were convinced by what they heard. Peter would have been using very poor judgment if he had gotten up before them when they cried out, "Men and brethren, what shall we do," if he had said: "Well, you have to hear the gospel, and you must believe the gospel." Friends, they had already been pricked in their hearts, so they must have heard what Peter said to them. They must have believed it, for they were pricked in their hearts. Now, what do we have altogether? They had heard the gospel, they had believed it, they were told to turn away from their sins, they were told to be baptized for the remission of their sins in order that they might receive the gift of the Holy Spirit. Now what is that? It is the oldest law of pardon.

Let us go on to Acts the 8th chapter for the next one. I will just give you several of the accounts of conversion in the New Testament and you can make a note of them and read them for yourselves. There are two accounts in the 8th chapter. One is the record of the conversion of the people in the city of Samaria. Philip went down to the city of Samaria and preached Christ to them. You have to preach Christ to people, friends, before they can accept the oldest law of pardon. You can tell a lot of graveyard yarns and get them scared; you can tell a lot of death-bed tales and stir up their emotions, and you can talk a lot about sweet moral philosophies and perhaps effect them to some extent, but if they ever obey the gospel of the Lord Jesus Christ they must hear the preaching of Jesus. Jesus has to be preached to them, because salvation is based upon the Lord Jesus Christ. Jesus is the one who died for our sins. The Bible says that Philip went down to the city of Samaria and preached Christ to them, and when he had preached Christ unto them, these people were greatly interested in all he said and did. Philip told them that they needed to accept that Lord and to turn away from their wickedness. When finally they did that, the Book says that they were baptized in the name of the Lord Jesus Christ. When they heard the preaching of the name of the Lord and the kingdom of heaven, "they were baptized both men and women," is exactly what the record says.

In the same 8th chapter of Acts, as Philip was going on his way, there was an Ethiopian eunuch coming from Jerusalem—he had been living in Africa under Queen Candace, as the ruler of her treasury—and was returning back home, having been up to Jerusalem worshipping under the old law. He was reading from the Old Testament, and Philip ran up to him and said: "Understandest thou what thou readest?" and he said, "How can I expect some man should guide me?" And he desired Philip to come up and sit with him, and the place of the scripture where he read was this: "He was led as a sheep to the slaughter; and like a lamb before his shearer, so he opened not his mouth: in his humiliation his judgment was taken away: and who shall declare his generation? for his life is taken from the earth." Then he turned to Philip and said to him: "Of whom speaketh the prophet this? of himself, or of some other man? Then Philip began at the same scripture and preached unto him Jesus. And as they went on their way, they came to a certain water: and the eunuch said, See, here is water; what doth hinder me to be baptized? He said, if thou believest with all thine heart, thou mayest. And the eunuch said, I believe that Jesus Christ is the Son of God. And he commanded the chariot to stand still: and they went down both into the water, both Philip and the eunuch; and he baptized him." Now what do we have there? The same thing as we have there (pointing to chart on Acts 2:38 on blackboard).

The 9th chapter of Acts is exactly the same, which is the record of Saul of Tarsus. He heard the gospel, believed the gospel and obeyed the gospel. As we see him walking and going about over the country and telling the story as a child of God, he frequently referred to his conversion. What happened to him? Jesus appeared to him on the way, but even Jesus didn't tell him what to do to be saved. He said: "Go into the city, and there it will be told you what you must do." Sometimes people say, "I thought Saul of Tarsus was saved out on the road to Damascus." Well, friends, he wasn't, because if he were he still had his sins on him. In the 22nd chapter of Acts and verse 16 the record says that Ananias said to Saul of Tarsus: "And now why tarriest thou? arise, and be baptized, and wash away thy sins, calling on the name of the Lord." The fact of the matter is, he didn't hear the gospel of Christ until he got into the city of Damascus, because the Lord simply told him to go into the city and there it would be told him what to do.

In Acts 10 we have the record of the conversion of Cornelius and his family. Cornelius sent for Peter; Peter came and preached the word to him; he heard the word, he believed it and obeyed it and that made him a Christian. In the 16th chapter of Acts we have two more records: one is of Lydia and her household and the other is the Philippian jailor. Lydia and her family likewise heard the gospel, believing it and obeyed it, and the Philippian jailor heard the same thing. Friends, I wouldn't mind taking anyone of them tonight and saying: "That is an example of Old Fashion Law of Pardon." If you have been wondering about such matters, then you read Acts 2, Acts 8, Acts 10 and Acts 16 and you will get the oldest law of pardon.

There is something else I want to mention. God at no time, for any purpose ever told a sinner who was on his knees, "Pray on, brother, and you will get salvation by and by." I was brought up in a community where the old "mourner's bench" type of salvation was preached on every hand. I have been out to the various denominations in the community where I used to live, in fact, we practiced in substance the same things at the Old Park Avenue Baptist Church for many years. I attended the Baptist Church for several years—although not a member—and we used to

practice such things except we were more up to date than
some of the Methodists and the Presbyterians about us, and
the Nazarenes just around the corner. We were just a
little more up to date. We had what we called an "inquiry
room." The sinners who came forward were taken out in
the "inquiry room" for their praying, etc., just a bit more
private than out in front of all the people in the building.
A long time ago nearly all denominations practiced the
mourner's bench type of salvation. Nearly all of them did.
(Very few do it that way today; we are just a little more
up to date.)

I remember hearing about an incident which happened
some time ago in a tent meeting. The preacher—the
evangelist—who had come in had waxed pretty warm in
his sermon, (just like I do sometimes you know) and he
was calling for "mourners," (except I don't do that). There
was a prominent doctor in the town, who happened to be
in the audience, and because I don't know his name I am
going to call him Dr. Anderson. Anyhow, the doctor had
attended the service once or twice previous to this. When
the preacher began calling for mourners and people were
kneeling down in the saw-dust praying for religion—praying for God to save them—Dr. Anderson came down and
he started to kneel down in the saw-dust. The preacher
reached over and said: "No, no, Doctor, it is not necessary
for you to get down in the saw-dust." Well, why not? If
that is the way the thing is done, why not? It doesn't
make any difference who a man is, God is no respector of
persons, "but in every nation he that feareth God and
worketh righteousness is accepted with him," and if that
is the way to do it, then the great doctor should have
gotten down too. It doesn't make any difference who he
is, doctor, lawyer, merchant, chief. If the law of pardon
demands that people get down in the saw-dust, why then
that is the way it ought to be done by all. But the truth
of the matter is, friends, that is not the way it is done in
the Bible. There isn't an example in the whole New Testament that God at any time, for any purpose, ever said to a

sinner on his knees, "Now then you just keep on praying and I will send my Holy Spirit and you will be saved and have an experience of grace, or something of that sort." Friends, the oldest law of pardon is the thing I want you to see tonight. The oldest law of pardon.

I am going to have to pass on or I will preach as long as I did last night. I want to get to the next one, and that is THE OLDEST FORM OF WORSHIP. Well, what do we mean by such an expression? Why we simply mean the things that God teaches in His word concerning worship which Christians should practice. That is important. What is worship? Worship is praise and adoration to God through any of the scriptural means provided in the word of God. We worship God in the reading and study of the Bible. We worship in prayer; in the singing praises unto God; when we engage in the contributing of our means; and of taking the Lord's Supper. Those are the five items of worship.

Now then, in any of these things, or in all of them, we worship God. In whatsoever we do in word or deed, we do it all in the name of the Lord, giving thanks unto God by him. So when I read the scriptures I am to read prayerfully. When I preach the gospel, I should preach fervently and prayerfully, and you should hear it prayerfully, and pray that the preacher may preach the truth and not error, preaching the word of God as God has delivered it. When we sing, we sing praises unto God and we pray in His name. I used to preach this sermon a great deal in North Carolina where the Christian Church and the Free Will Baptist Church were very strong, and I would often times get an invitation to preach in one of the local Christian Churches in that community. There are a lot of members of the Christian Church in North Carolina, possibly several hundred congregations in that part of the state, the eastern part of North Carolina. I have preached in some of the Christian Churches in that community with the understanding that I would be permitted to conduct the song service. I would try to be as nice as I could. I told them that I would not take advantage of the place they had given me and be ugly or rude. (I am never ugly and rude). I know that I must stand before God and give an account for the way that I preach, my very demeanor. I love the souls of men, brother. I don't want to be rude to anybody. If I am rude to somebody, and intentionally drive that fellow away where he will never let me have another opportunity to preach to him, why of course that would be wrong. My demeanor should be such that would characterize love and concern for souls.

Well I would say: "I would like to come and preach." When I got there I would preach this sermon invariably: "Old Fashion Religion." The oldest church. The oldest law of pardon. You would see some of those old people out in the congregation who had not heard it made that plain in some time, nudge each other—"This fellow is really preaching the truth." The oldest church—you would see them exchange glances in appreciation for the things I would say. But friends, when I would get down to this point: The oldest form of worship, I would talk about the Lord's Supper; I would talk about the contribution; I would talk about the prayer; I would talk about the reading of the scriptures, and then I would talk about the kind of music that was to be made in worship unto the Lord. That would be the place that we would disagree.

I said last night, or night before last, that I am not prejudiced against instrumental music. The reason that I don't use it in the worship is because God doesn't authorize it. I am not prejudiced against it. I love the sweet strains of a pipe organ, and I love to hear a piano well played. I am very fond of instrumental music. But the reason I can't use it in worship is because God doesn't authorize it in the oldest form of worship. Now let me read this for you. In Matthew 26:30 and Mark 14:26 the record says: "And when they had sung an hymn, they went out in the mount of Olives." In the 16th chapter of the Acts of Apostles and the 25th verse: "Paul and Silas sang praises unto God at midnight and the prisoners heard them." In Romans

15:9 Paul says, "I will confess to thee among the Gentiles, and sing unto thy name." In I Corinthians 14:15: "I will sing with the spirit, and I will sing with the understanding also." In Ephesians 5:19 it reads: "Speaking to yourselves in Psalms and hymns and spiritual songs, singing and making melody in your heart to the Lord." Colossians 3:16 says : "Teaching and admonishing one another in psalms and hymns and spiritual songs, singing with grace in your hearts to the Lord." In Hebrews 2:12: "In the midst of the church will I sing praise unto you." In James 5:13: "Is any merry? let him sing psalms."

I have read every one of the nine passages of scripture in the New Testament on the subject of the song service, the worship unto God in song as recorded in the oldest form of worship for the Christian. Listen, brethren and friends, I want you to know that every one of them states that the kind of music made was the kind that we make with our voices and our hearts. Don't ever make the mistake, my good friends, of going out and saying that the people of the church of Christ are prejudiced against mechanical instrumental music. That is not true, and you ought not to make that statement, if you have ever made it, and I'm sure nobody here ever has. I want you to see the position that we really advocate is that we do not use mechanical instruments in the worship because God has not authorized it in His word.

Take the Lord's Supper as mentioned in Matthew 26:17-30: "Jesus took bread and blessed it and brake it, and gave it to his disciples and said, Take, eat: this is my body, and he took the cup, and gave thanks and gave it to them saying, Drink ye all of it." Now, what elements did Jesus use in instituting the Lord's Supper that night? He used bread—unleaven bread—and the fruit of the vine. My friends, you see how the Lord instituted it? He stipulated the things that we are to use on it by his own example. No one would ever dream of violating His will by going beyond, putting something else on the Lord's Table that the Lord has not authorized. Very well, why should I then

do something in the song service which God has not
authorized just because it pleases me? I have had people to
use that argument. "Oh, Brother Pickup, I understand
that we don't have a direct reference to instrumental music
in the New Testament, I understand that, but it is so satis-
fying to the people, it is so soothing. Anything that pleases
people so much, and is so quieting to the nerves, must be
pleasing unto God." Let me say this to you, friends: How
do you know that something that pleases man will please
God who has never been a man? You can't decide what will
please God on the basis of what pleases man. The people
were pleased with the making of the golden calf, but it
didn't please God. You couldn't say on that basis that we
could have instrumental music in New Testament worship.
Let us think this thing through, friends. That is what I
am trying to get you to do tonight: just think it through
and see for ourselves what is taught in the oldest law of
Christian worship.

The matter of the contribution, how is that to be done?
The Bible says "Upon the first day of the week let every
one of you lay by him in store, as God hath prospered him,
that there be no gatherings when I come." That is I Corinthians 16:2. The first verse says: "As I gave order to
the churches of Galatia, so also do ye." You know, sometimes a man will stand behind the Lord's table and after
we have taken the Lord's Supper, and he insists that we
ought to do it because the Bible says so, and that is right;
he says, when he comes to the contribution: "Now then,
brethren, this is a gracious privilege that we have of giving." Privilege nothing, it is an order! Paul said: "AS
I GAVE ORDER unto the churches in Galatia, even so do
ye." I don't know how he would make it any stronger, but
the brethren seem to be a little timid about the contribution, because of the fact that, with some, when you touch
their pocketbooks you touch them in a mighty sensitive
spot. I don't know why this is true, but it is sometimes.
I want to tell you, friends, the contribution is an order!
There will be a lot of people go to hell because they haven't

obeyed the gospel teaching with reference to the giving of their means as God has prospered them. I would be ashamed to come before God in the judgment having violated that part of the oldest form of worship. I want to go a step further than that: many people who are in the church of the Lord Jesus Christ, who are members of the one body, who condemn the denominations and correctly so, because they use mechanical instruments of music in the worship and, therefore, have added to God's divine will, are themselves guilty of a sin just as serious by their failure to give to the Lord as they have been prospered. The stingy member of the church who refuses to give of his means as God has prospered him is going just as deep into hell as the fellow who adds to the teaching of God's divine will. When you come before Him in the judgment, you are going to have to stand there to give an account for the way you use your money in the service of the Lord, or have left it in the bank or in an investment, or have improperly used it to the gratification of your own flesh.

Now then, friends, I want you to see one other point that I want to make with reference to THE OLDEST NAME. Old fashion religion demands not only the oldest church, the oldest law of pardon, the oldest form of Christian worship, but likewise the oldest name. What is the name that I am referring to? Well let me read the passages. In the 11th chapter of the Book of the Acts of Apostles and verse 26. "The disciples were called Christians first at Antioch."

I heard a man say one time that the name "Christian" was given in derision. Do you know that there is one important thing wrong with that? It just isn't so. There isn't a thing in the Bible that indicates it anywhere. I want to give you the exact meaning of it. That word "Called"— and the disciples "were called" Christians first at Antioch —comes from the Greek word *kramatidso*, which has absolutely no idea of calling in derision, but actually has reference to exactly the opposite. In the passive voice, Thayer says: ". . . to teach from heaven," and ". . . . receive a name, or title, to be called." There is certainly no grounds for saying they were called "Christians" in derision. So don't ever make that mistake. The Bible says that "the disciples were CALLED Christians first at Antioch."

Friends, don't you see that if that is the name God gave, it is the name that you and I ought to wear today? In the 6th chapter of Acts of Apostles and the 28th verse the Bible says that this man Agrippa, the king, said: "Almost thou persuadest me to be a Christian." And then over here in I Peter 4:16: "Yet if any man suffer as a Christian, let him not be ashamed, but let him glorify God on this behalf." The American Standard Version says: "In this name."

My friends, "Christian" is the name that God has given to His people, and we wear that name, and we wear it to the exclusion of any other name. Well, do you mean that you do not have any other name? Oh, yes, we have other names. Well, what are they? "Saint" is one of the names of God's people. Suppose that I were to stand up here tonight and say: "After the service is over, saint Cope (one of the elders) will dismiss the congregation." I would be using a scriptural expression. Do you know that S-A-I-N-T, as used in the Bible, never did refer to a dead person who has been canonized, as taught by the Roman Catholic Church and a few other religious groups? Such has no connection with the Bible, like most of the teachings of the Roman Catholics. Saint is a name of God's people.

Here is another one: "Disciple." We use that name too, and we also use the name "brother" or "brethren." When I refer to the church which Jesus built, I call it the "church of Christ," or the "church of the Lord," or the "church of God," or simply the "church." Such expressions are used to designate the oldest church and the members of the oldest church.

Thus, we follow the oldest law of pardon; we have the oldest form of worship; we wear the oldest name. All the other names that denominate people in one way or another, that refer to the act of baptism such as the "Baptist Church" or "Baptists," or to refer to the government such as "Methodists," "Presbyterians," etc., are not old. They are not as old as the New Testament. The Bible states that the name of the members of the New Testament church was the name "Christian." The only people ever referred to in the Bible by the name "Christian" were those individuals so designated by the inspired writings as being members of the New Testament church.

Now there is one more. Old fashion religion teaches man he should follow the OLDEST CREED. What is it? Why, it is the New Testament. We do not have some other creed. We don't have some other form that tells what we believe, but this is the creed. (Holds up Bible). Let me read it for you. II Timothy 3:16,17: "All scripture is given by inspiration of God, and is profitable for doctrine, for reproof, for correction, for instruction in righteousness: that the man of God may be perfect, throughly furnished unto all good works." The American Standard Version says: "that the man of God may be complete, furnished completely unto every good work." Many other passages refer to the word of God as the authority, yea, the *creed* of those who followed the Lord. If the "scriptures" of God are sufficient to make man complete, then he needs no modern creed, confession of faith, church manual—or what have you—to guide him. The oldest church used the scriptures as they were spoken by men of God in New Testament times, who were moved by the Holy Spirit. Members of that oldest church today follow the same Spirit-guided words as they have been written in the New Testament. Therefore, the oldest creed is the inspired word of God as written in the New Testament itself.

Friends, do you want to be a member of the oldest church—the one built by Jesus Christ? I am not asking you to "join" anything tonight, but I am simply asking you to submit to the oldest law of pardon. And when you do, the Lord will add you to the church of the New Testament, the oldest church. Then you are to follow the way of the Lord in the oldest form of worship, as recorded in the oldest creed. Then wear the oldest name, which is also recorded in the New Testament.

In conclusion tonight, let me say if you want Old Fashion Religion, then you want New Testament Christianity. That is what I am asking you to accept tonight, and when you do it, the Lord will add you to the church. Are you a subject of the invitation? Have you been thinking about it? Have you been pondering these truths at some time or another? Then why not reconsider and say, "Tonight will be just as good a time as any," and come to the front, give Brother Phillips your hand and give God your heart; obey his will and be faithful unto death? One day God will give you a home over there to live with Him throughout the ages of eternity. Will you come, while together we stand and sing?

INDIVIDUAL RESPONSIBILITY

We come to the last service of this meeting, as Brother Phillips suggested, with a feeling of regret that the meeting is about over. We always enjoy making new friends, meeting old friends, preaching the gospel to people that we have not preached to before, and enjoying together the fellowship of the saints of the Lord. But we come to the concluding service of the meeting tonight.

I have just a few words to say before I get into my lesson that I have reserved to say until tonight. One of them deals with the fact that there is a person who is missing from this meeting, but who is conspicious by his absence. If it were possible, that person would have been here during every one of these services. He was here during the last meeting that I conducted in this building, and I have missed him greatly during this campaign for the saving of souls. That person is our beloved Elder Phillips who has not been here for some months now, but was taken away by death as most of you already know. The memory of this great man continues to linger. He was worth so much to the Cause—not only here, but everywhere. I loved him because of his great love for the truth, his genial personality, and I am sure that you, as well as I, shall miss him very much.

Another thing that I want to say, and that is to express to all of you my appreciation for the many kindnesses that you have expressed to me during the time that I have been here in this meeting. In fact, not only at this time, but all other times that I have been privileged to be in your company. I am grateful for the many kindnesses which you have extended to me, the opportunities that I have had of being in your home and eating your food, and enjoying myself generally with your hospitality. I never know how to say that I appreciate these matters, but I do want you to know that I am grateful for all of them. I have enjoyed this meeting very much; working with these elders and deacons and this fine gospel preacher, Brother Phillips, whom I have known for several years has been a real pleasure. It is a great inspiration to me to know that there are men who love the truth and who will stand for the truth, and will not get up behind sermons that I preach, or that some other preacher preaches, and apologize for them. I appreciate that very much. I am grateful for the many, many pleasant associations that I have had with Brother and Sister Phillips, now and in times past and gone. I only hope that it will be my privilege to labor again with him in any capacity, for I am sure that any capacity in which he labors will be one that God will approve. I appreciate the fine work that he and all the other members of this congregation are doing.

Then there is something else that I want to say tonight that I indulge myself in sometimes. They tell me that you do these things as you get older, and I have reference to thinking retrospectively. The person that I am going to mention doesn't have any idea that I am going to say this, and he doesn't know what I am going to say. In fact, neither do you (and that isn't unusual), but the thing that I mean is that I want to say a few words thinking back about 27 years ago when I first started my work as a gospel preacher. Brother W. A. Cameron is here tonight. This is the first time that he has been able to come to the meeting. I don't know whether he remembers it or not, the exact date, but I am sure he has got it down somewhere and I would like for him to look up the date. It has been, Brother Cameron, almost exactly 27 years to the day when I stood up in the little congregation over on Ninth Street and made my first talk as a gospel preacher. I would not have done it I'm sure except for the insistence of W. A. Cameron. I want to say this in his presence, as I have it before, I do not know anyone for whom I have greater respect. This is because of his loyalty to the truth, his courage in its presentation, and the fact that he has been zealous in his labors in the Cause of the Lord Jesus. It could possibly have been that another man would be standing in this pulpit tonight in your meeting, had it not been for the efforts of our

Brother Cameron. He and I are are pretty much about the same age with respect to the days: his birthday is on the 14th of August and mine is on the 9th. I am six days older than he, in days, but he is 30 years older than I, in years. So if you happen to know that he is in his 82nd year, then you know that I am in my 52nd.

I just wanted to make these remarks in view of the fact that he is present tonight. I am not dishing out some taffy to him or making undue or undeserved remarks or compliments; I just wanted to give "honor to whom honor is due" in view of the fact that tonight is almost exactly 27 years since I preached my first gospel sermon. I don't know how good I did that night, and I have forgotten what my sermon was, but I hope I haven't forgotten the one that I am going to preach tonight.

I want to read now as a background for some of the things that I want to say, in the 14th chapter of the book of Romans and beginning at verse 8: "For whether we live, we live unto the Lord; and whether we die, we die unto the Lord: whether we live therefore, or die, we are the Lord's. For to this end Christ both died, and rose, and revived, that he might be Lord both of the dead and living. But why dost thou judge thy brother? or why dost thou set at nought thy brother? for we shall all stand before the judgment seat of Christ. For it is written, As I live, saith the Lord, every knee shall bow to me, and every tongue shall confess to God. So then every one of us shall give account of himself to God." That is the reading from Romans 14:8-12. I have the American Standard Version open before me on the table, and I shall read from both of these as we talk to you tonight about *Individual Responsibility*.

I believe that such a sermon as this is fitting for the close of a gospel meeting. I have preached it dozens and dozens of times and if I live long enough I expect to preach it many, many more. I try to think that God in His infiinite wisdom and mercy has made it possible that I could come under the influence of the gospel of Christ, and that I have had opportunity to learn His truth and obey His will. I am grateful for the fact that God was long-suffering to me and that He gave me opportunity after opportunity to hear and to believe and obey the gospel. One day I marched down the aisle, gave the preacher my hand and said, "I want to be a Christian." I have tried to live true and faithful to that through the years, but I am conscious continually of the responsibility that rests upon me as I talked to people about the gospel of the Lord Jesus Christ. My friends, there are other passages that I desire to call to your attention, and one of them is the statement made by Paul when he said: "Woe is me if I preach not the gospel of the Lord Jesus Christ." He also said: "I buffet my body and bring it into subjection, lest when I have preached to others, I myself should be a castaway." So you can see that responsibility continues on and on and the older a person gets, the more he grows, spiritually, and the more constant he may be in possession of opportunities, the greater his responsibilities continue to be. So as you grow older in the work of the Lord, more capable in His service after the years have gone by and you are getting older and more acquainted with the gospel of Christ, then your responsibilities will continue to be heavier. If you are not better acquainted with the gospel of Christ as the years go by, then you are falling down on your responsibility and God is going to hold you accountable.

I am looking at a passage in Luke the 24th chapter, verses 46, 47 which is, as you recall, one of the recitations of the great commission. He says: "Thus it is written, and thus it behooved Christ to suffer, and to rise from the dead the third day: and that repentance and remission of sins might be preached in his name among all nations, beginning from Jerusalem." Now my point in reading that is this: that the Lord Jesus Christ said in that passage that ALL MEN ARE RESPONSIBLE! You cannot escape responsibility unless you are in one of two classifications: if you do not have the faculty of reasoning—have not the mind with which to think—or you have not reached the age of accountability unto God. I know that there are no other classes because the Bible includes all people in its demands, except the two mentioned. So all men everywhere are responsible. That is a tremendous thing, my friends. It is a staggering thought to realize that everybody must give an account of himself to God. That is the thing that I want to keep before you tonight. There are some things that only you can do; and there are some things that only you can say; there are some people that only you can reach with the gospel of the Lord Jesus Christ.

But I want you to notice a statement that is made here which I read a moment ago. The Bible says, "Everyone of us shall give an account of himself unto God." Now then the one to whom I am to give an account is the Lord. You are not responsible in the great judgment unto me, but you are responsible to the Lord God of heaven. That makes it still more serious. You know, we can get by with men. Sometimes we can talk people out of rendering a decision against us, as is frequently done in the court rooms of our land, but you can't get up before the Lord in the judgment and even plead your own case, because the judgment day is not a time of the hearing of evidences. Such is not the purpose of judgment day. Judgment day is the day of rendering the decision and passing the judgment upon the evidence that has already been presented. The Book says that everyone shall give an account of himself, not argue his case. There is not going to be any arguing of the case before the Lord in the judgment, and the examples that we will use will show conclusively that this is true.

Actually we are responsible not only to God on behalf of ourselves, but we are responsible likewise on behalf of our fellowman. Paul said in Romans 1:14: "I am debtor both to the Greeks, and to the Barbarians; both to the wise, and to the unwise. So, as much as in me is, I am now ready to preach the gospel to you that are at Rome also." You can see, friends, that we are responsible unto God first and foremost, but we have a responsibility to our neighbors and friends. We must not lead them astray. We must not live a bad example before them, but we must live a good example before our neighbors and friends. We have a responsibility and an obligation even to those who are outside the family of God. We have a third responsibility, friends, and that is to the church of the living God. I am a member of the body of Christ and I must consider my calling and my election as a member of that body, and I must consider my brethren who are citizens of the kingdom of God because I have an influence over them.

The Bible contains many expressions to the effect that we must not hinder the weak brethren, but we must consider them and help them not to stumble. And if I can save a brother from the error of his way, then that conduct will cover a multitude of sins: his sins, if you please. You can see, therefore, that responsibility is important and we need to think about it. We are going to try and get a little bit closer to it. I have just surveyed the points in the introduction and I hope you will follow each one closely.

First of all, I want to speak with regard to: "WHAT ARE THE RESPONSIBILITIES? Or rather among the classifications of individuals, what is the responsibility of the various ones? Suppose I take the first one. The alien sinner; what is that individual's responsibility? The Bible teaches that there are several things that he needs to think about. I am going to read one that doesn't cover that, but it is an argument to show that the alien sinner is responsible. In II Thess. 1:7, 8: "And to you who are troubled rest with us, when the Lord Jesus shall be revealed from heaven with his mighty angels, in flaming fire taking vengeance on them that know not God, and that obey not the gospel of our Lord Jesus Christ." And then in Hebrews 5:8, 9: "Though he were a Son, yet learned he obedience by the things which he suffered; and being made perfect, he became the author of eternal salvation unto all them that obey him." This refers to the one outside the covenant relationship with Christ who failed to obey the first principles of the gospel of Christ. I have read that with this in mind: I want you to see, my friends, that if you are not a member of the body of Christ—and when I say that I mean if you are not a member of the church of the New Testament—you are some day going to answer to God for that fact. Now I have talked to you evening after evening about the church of the New Testament. I have tried to point out what it is, that it was an organization that was founded by the Lord and not by man; that it has a divine name, not a denominational or human name; that it has a divine plan, not a human plan; that it is a divine organization, not a human organization. As much as we love the various things that are about us, as much confidence as we have in individuals and in cities and nations and other institutions in the world, the church of the living God is the most important institution on the face of God's earth. The reason for that is because Jesus built the church to contain the saved, hence everyone is going to be held accountable for the fact that he is or is not a member of that organization. Now I want you to think about that before I pass on. I want you to recognize the fact that what I am saying is very important; that if you are a member of some human organization, or not a member of anything, for that matter, then you need to do something about responsibility number one. That is your obligation and that is the thing that you are going to find yourself facing in the judgment. Suppose you come before Him in that great day and you try to present your case. You say to Jesus: "Lord, Lord, didn't I do this and didn't I do that and didn't I do the other. All things you "didn't" do. We have an example somewhat similar in Matthew 7:21-25. This fellow told all he had done, but the Lord didn't know him. He had done a lot, but he had not done anything to make the Lord know who he was. You know, sometimes people say: "Well, don't I have a right to believe my own way? and don't I have a right to my own opinion?" Here is a fellow who didn't. He didn't have a right to his opinion when he crossed the teaching of the Lord. While he said: "Lord, Lord, it is my opinion that I have been prophesying and teaching and working and acting in your name; and yet you say you don't know anything about me?" Listen, friends, that was his responsibility. He was coming before the Lord in that day being held accountable, not for the fact that he didn't visit the fatherless and widows in their afflictions, but because he was not known by the Lord. Now helping the unfortunate in their afflictions might come up with someone else. This man, however, was not being condemned for not taking the Lord's Supper. He was not held accountable for not doing the work of a Christian. He was held responsible, or accountable, for the fact that he was not known by the Lord. Well, who does the Lord know? Why He knows His own. The Lord knoweth them that are his; and let every one that nameth the name of the Lord depart from iniqiuity. That statement is made by Paul to Timothy in II Timothy 2:19. Thus the Lord knows them that are his. Why didn't the Lord know that fellow in Matthew 7 who said: "Lord, Lord," don't you know me? And the Lord said, "I don't know you." It was because he was not the Lord's own. That is the reason. The Lord knoweth them that are His. You don't need to worry about that. The Lord knows them that belong to Him.

I lived across the river from Washington, D. C. for six years. It is an education to live in Washington, and I had some very interesting experiences while there. You will remember that for several years I lived in Florida prior to going to the Washington area, and became acquainted with a lot of people here. Among them I met one of our representatives to Congress. Well, while down here where he was canvassing for votes, of course he was pretty genial and knew just about everybody he met, at least he gave you that impression of himself. After I moved to Washington, one day I thought to myself: "I think I will just stop in and see our representative from Florida." You are supposed to send in your card—I didn't have one—but I wrote my name on one that was provided for that purpose. Pretty soon he came out and shook hands with me and made some genial remarks. I was one of his constituents, so to speak, at least he felt that way about it, but I could tell that it was all just on the surface; he didn't know me at all. Later when I came in contact with him on another occasion, under different circumstances, he just didn't know me. I didn't take any exceptions to that. I don't expect a man like a congressman to recognize me from the other hundreds and thousands of people that he comes in contact with. But my point, my friends, is this: sometimes you will see somebody that doesn't know you when you really think he should because of something you have done, hence to you such is quite important.

But you just think how important it is if you get up before the Lord in the judgment and the Lord says, "You will have to go somewhere else, Bud, I never knew you." That IS going to be serious. That is going to be serious. I am saying all that, friends, to say this: You have to accept your responsibility and do the will of the Lord concerning your obligation or you are never going to be saved at last. People can say this or that or the other, and tell you to do this and that, and tell you to follow the ways that you have been going, where your good old mother and good old father went, but one of these days you are going to have to face this thing in the judgment. If you are not in that kingdom then you are an alien sinner and you will be looked upon as an outsider because you will not be a member of the Lord's church.

Well, what is the responsibility of the alien sinner? You remember last night I read from Acts the 2nd chapter. Acts the 8th chapter, Acts the 9th chapter, Acts the 10th and 16th chapter and other passages which show the responsibility of the alien. Tonight I want to put them down on the blackboard that you may see them plainly. First of all, the sinner is going to be held responsible for hearing the gospel of the Lord Jesus Christ. You can say: "Well, if I don't hear it I will be all right." No you won't! You are responsible for hearing it. God is holding you responsible for hearing the gospel of Christ. The first

commandment is to "hear, Oh Israel." **You are going to**
have to hear the gospel yourself.   Mark 12:29 is the
passage that I just quoted.   You must hear the word of
the Lord.   The people on the day of Pentecost, those who
had received his word, were those who had heard, because
Peter was talking to them on that occasion.   Not only must
you hear but you must believe the word of the Lord Jesus
Christ.   You must believe that word that has been presented.   You must believe truth and not error.   You know
belief is important, but it is not believing that saves a man.
Now you will probably say, "I heard you say in this meeting that man is saved by faith."   Well, that is right with
respect to what I was talking about in that sermon, but I
am saying to you now: It is not believing that saves a man.
What is it?   It is WHAT he believes.   If he believes error,
that will damn his soul.

There are a lot of people who are believers: they believe
error, and they are going to hell because they believe error.
It is not believing that will save a man.   It is not eating
that makes a man fat, it is WHAT he eats.   If he eats
sawdust, do you reckon he will get fat?   You heard of the
fellow who tried to fatten his mule on sawdust didn't you?
He kept adding a little more sawdust and a little more
sawdust to the feed that he was giving him, until by and
by the old mule wasted away because sawdust was about
all he was getting.   (Maybe I need to eat a little sawdust.)
The point that I want you to get is that it is not eating
that makes one fat or gives him the muscle that he needs,
it is WHAT he eats.   You know that is true.   You can
understand that even if you never thought about it before.
It is not believing that will save you, brother, it is WHAT
you believe.   The Bible says the Devils believe and tremble.
They believe and they tremble, but the fact that you believe
is not important beyond the fact that it is a part of your
overt act in the matter.   But the important thing is
WHAT you believe.   You have to believe the truth; you
have to believe what the Bible says—what the gospel says
—in order to be saved.

A few years ago while living in Arlington, Virginia there was a man who came into our company one Sunday morning, who had previously been shot down over the South Pacifiic. His name was Musick—Ken Musick—he was a commander in the U. S. Navy. He had bailed out of a Navy plane that was going down into the great, vast ocean. When he hit the water, the little life raft opened up and he began to look around and see some of the things with which he could take care of himself, for he didn't know how long he would be there. He said one of the things that came out as he began to scramble around was a Bible, a little Testament. He said when he picked it up, it just flopped itself open at the 13th chapter of Hebrews. Well, that Sunday morning when he marched into the Arlington church building, somebody handed him a Bible, because the Sunday morning Bible class was just about ready to start, and it was opened to the 13th chapter of Hebrews. He just sat down in his seat and took up where he had started back yonder on the Pacific some months before. During the mnoths that followed, Ken Musick heard the gospel, believed the gospel and finally obeyed the gospel, but he had asked me question after question before he eventually accepted the truth. That Sunday evening he went home with me from services and he said: "The only reason I came," (he was a member of the Congregational Church) "was because I promised a man that I met in the Navy who was a member of the church of Christ, that I would investigate the church of Christ and what they believe as the truth of God. That is the reason that I am here. I am interested all right, but I want to tell you that I must see the evidence before I believe it." Commander Musick realized that believing was important all right, but that WHAT you believe is very important. So we began to study, and evening after evening we would be together. It took him some 30 days possibly and I imagine we had a dozen or more sessions with him—because he could ask more questions than nearly anybody I ever saw —but he said in substance, "I want to know because I want to believe, not what you think about it, or some other preacher thinks about it, but I want to believe what God wants me to know." I said one thing to him then, what I have said to many others before and since and I want to say it to you tonight: Every time you open the Book and begin to read it, say to yourself: "What does God want me to know about this that I am reading? Not what do I want to know that will please me? or what can I find that will justify the position I have already taken? What does God want me to know." That, my friends, is the important thing, namely: what you believe. If you believe error you can be lost, but if you believe truth, then the words of truth will guide you into His will and you will obey it and go to heaven when life is over. So hearing is important and the alien sinner must hear; he must hear the truth. The alien sinner also must believe; he must believe the truth. Another thing he must do is repent of his sins. The Bible teaches that unless you repent you shall all likewise perish. You have to turn away from error, from evil, from those things that are wrong, and that is repentance —turning away from those things.

Jesus also said: "Whoso shall confess me before men, him will I confess before my Father which is in heaven." Therefore, I want to put that down too. I haven't mentioned the confession except a time or two in passing, but I want to say something about it tonight. What is the confession? Well, I want to read it to you. The Bible says: "Whoso shall confess me before men, him will I also confess before my Father which is in heaven." And then we read in Romans 10:10: "With the heart man believeth unto righteousness, and with the mouth confession is made unto salvation." What do you confess? You must confess the Lord Jesus Christ. Don't make the mistake of confessing something else. Practically every denomination calls upon the candidates for baptism to make some arrangement of the following: the question is asked: "Do you believe that God for Christ's sake has pardoned your sins?" and the person is expected to say, "Yes." Well, I want to tell you, friends, that no New Testament preacher ever asked a sinner such a question—it is not in the Bible. "Do you believe that God for Christ's sake has pardoned your sins?" Answering such a question before he has been baptized for the remission of sins (Acts 2:38) is one of the reasons why, even though that individual might have been immersed in the name of the Father, and of the Son and of the Holy Spirit, the immersion is not valid because the act was done presuming that the individual's sins were already remitted before the person was baptized. Now I hope you can see that such a confession is not the confession of Jesus.

In the 8th chapter of the book of Acts, verses 36, 37, 38, as Philip and the eunuch were going along, they came to a certain water and the eunuch said: "See, here is water, what doth hinder me to be baptized?" And Philip said, "If thou believeth with all thine heart, thou mayest. And he answered and said, I believe that Jesus Christ is the Son of God. And he commanded the chariot to stand still: and they went down both into the water, both Philip and the eunuch: and he baptized him."

What did he do? He confessed the Lord before men. That is the confession that God expects people to make. And after he confessed Christ he was baptized into Christ. Now what did that do for him? That put him IN the Lord, or IN CHRIST, and to be in Christ is to be in his church. The body is his church, Ephesians 1:22, 23, hence to be in Christ is to be in the body; the body is the church. You get into Christ by being baptized into Christ, therefore, you get into the church the same way. Well, what is the alien sinner's responsibility? He must hear the gospel, believe it, repent of his sins, confess Christ and be baptized.

Well, let us pass on to still another. I am looking at II Peter the first chapter, verses 5 and 7. This person mentioned here is not an alien sinner, but he is already a Christian. He has obeyed the gospel, because when he does that it puts him into Christ and makes him a child of God or a Christian. Does he have a responsibility? Yes he does. Listen to this statement. "And besides this," Peter says, "giving all diligence, add to your faith virtue; and to virtue knowledge; and to knowledge temperance; and to temperance patience; and to patience godliness; and to godliness brotherly kindness; and to brotherly kindness charity." What do you have as a responsibility, my brother, my sister, AFTER you become a Christian? One of them is to add these Christian graces to your faith. Add to your faith, knowledge, temperance, patience, godliness, brotherly kindness and love. Add them to your faith.

Then Peter makes another statement, and this is the last one he makes, in the 3rd chapter and verse 18 of the second letter where he says: "Grow in grace and in the knowledge of our Lord and Saviour Jesus Christ." What does God want me to do with reference to my responsibility as a child of God? I need, first of all, to add the Christian graces to my life; and then I need to grow in grace and in the knowledge of my Lord and Master Jesus Christ.

What does it mean to grow? Oh, friends, one of the reasons why so many members of the church fall away is because they have failed to grow and develop as Christians. I have had members of the church to tell me: "There is one thing I have neglected and that is, I am not quite as faithful as I ought to be, and I just don't go to church as I should." I have heard members say those things, and I have even heard some say it in a boastful manner. Well, friends, people who are not doing their duty in fulfilling their obligations as Christians are not carrying their responsibility. Do you often wonder why it is that many of them fall? Well they do, and it is because of the fact that they are walking along pretty close to the world all the time. Pretty soon they will lose their identity as Christians because they are so close to the things of the world, and had rather be there than to be engaging in the walk of the Lord.

I remember a little illustration some years ago that you may have heard. It is the story of a little girl whose mother put her to bed one evening—her bedroom was on the floor above the room where the mother was sitting. She took the little girl up to bed, put her in bed, and by and by the child was asleep. The mother was sitting in the room down stairs reading and sewing or doing something and suddenly she heard a heavy thud on the floor. She ran upstairs because she knew that the child had fallen out of bed, or at least she thought so, and when he got up there, sure enough the baby had fallen out of bed. The child was crying and the mother wiped away the tears. The little girl could talk fairly well, and she said to her: "Mary, how in the world did it happen? How did you happen to fall out of bed?" She said: "Mommie, I guess I was too near the getting in place."

I am sure that is true with regard to some of God's children. We stay too near to the world; we stay too close to the things of the world; and pretty soon, because we stay too near to the place where we came in—out of the world into the church—we sometimes fall by the wayside and lose ourselves in the great world of sin that is round about us. Now my point is, brethren and friends, that you as a child of God need to recognize your responsibility as a Christian: be faithful and loyal, worship God regularly, faithfully, loyally, doing His bidding, giving of your means and using yourselves in His service, because God wants you to add to your faith, and He wants you to grow in grace.

But I want you to notice one other principle I want to suggest to you, and this perhaps will be the last one tonight. I want to ask the question, friends, if we can see our own responsibilities? Men sometimes say: "I can't do this and I can't do that and I can't do something else, and you know God is not going to hold me accountable for doing things that I can't do." Well, that is right. God is not going to hold you accountable for doing something that you can't do, but He may hold you accountable for not learning to do it! He may hold you accountable for that. You need to develop yourself and I need to develop myself for being more useful as the days go by. Thus the responsibility of each of us.

Looking here at the blackboard we see the following:

1. THE ALIEN'S RESPONSIBILITY.
2. THE CHRISTIAN'S RESPONSIBILITY.
3. AM I SHOULDERING MY RESPONSIBILITY?

Am I shouldering my responsibility? I can't bear your obligation for you; you can't bear mine for me. We must each bear our own, because the Bible says so. But my point is: Are we shouldering OUR responsibilities?

A few years ago I met a man who at that time was a guard in the State Prison in Nashville. He was not a member of the church, but he had a wife and daughter who were members of the church. I had seen him in the services several times. I had preached to him about being a Christian, but this was the first time that I had talked to him privately about it. I thought he was getting interested and that soon he would obey the gospel, but when I talked to him, he made this statement to me: "Now listen, Brother Pickup, I appreciate you and I like to hear you preach and all of that, but my wife and daughter do my church going for me!" Well now, can a person do that for someone else? Can somebody else shoulder your responsibility for you? No, friends, they cannot. Nobody can carry mine. I must carry my own and you must carry your own. Now here is my passage. In Romans 14: 11, 12, the place where we started this discussion tonight: "For it is written, As I live, saith the Lord, every knee shall bow to me, and every tongue shall confess to God. So then every one of us shall give account of HIMSELF to God." Yours is yours and mine is mine. The question is: Am I shouldering my part of the load? Am I taking care of my part of the responsibility? I know that you know it is an individual matter. You have to study individually for yourself; you have to learn individually for yourself; and then when you learn, you have to obey individually for yourself.

I see many people about me that are not Christians. They are fine people who are not following the way of the Lord. Maybe they are religious, some of them are—many of them are men and women that I know, who are not members of the body of Christ. Although they may be very religious, they are not going to be saved, because they could not, to save their souls, read from God's divine will what they are doing in the name of Christ. As I notice such people I am concerned about them. Some of them are my people in the flesh. My mother and father were not members of the body of Christ. Don't you know that I would have been very happy to see those nearest to me obey the gospel before they died? But I wasn't successful in leading them to Christ, although I tried vainly to do so. My father heard me preach only three times in his life. He wasn't prejudiced against my preaching necessarily, but he was so steeped in agnosticism that he couldn't tear himself loose from his unbelief and he died out of Christ in spite of the fact that I think I did everything in my power up to almost the day of his death to bring him to the Lord. And my blessed mother who likewise died out of Christ, I asked her just a short time before her death if she wouldn't let me read something from the Bible to her. It was my hope that, even though she was very sick at the time, she might yet turn to the Lord and obey the gospel. She said, "Yes, I believe I would like it all right, if you would read something." I opened the Bible and began to read what I thought she needed to hear. And as I read, she may or may not have recognized some of the passages we had discussed through the years. But whether she realized what I was reading or just grew weary, she turned her face over to the wall and refused to listen.

One day we are all going to stand before the King in judgment. But, friends, listen: don't you know that if it were possible I would like to help my dear mother in the judgment day? She will be there in the judgment. She took her life in her hands to give me an existence into the world. She went to the very bar of death itself to give me birth in this world, and I am ever grateful for the fact that she loved me enough to bear me, to take care of me when I couldn't take care of myself, to watch over me and keep me from stumbling and to help me when I did stumble. Don't you know I would do everything in my power to help her in the judgment? But I can't help her. She is going to have to give her own account to God, and I'm going to have to give mine in the judgment. You must give your account in the judgment too.

A few years ago in the city of Boston, Massachusetts a young man about 19 or 20 years of age was being tried for murder. The jury had heard the evidence—it was a terrible crime, the manner in which it was committed and all of that. The jury went out and considered the evidence that they had heard, and it wasn't long until they came back and the man who was in charge of the jury stood up and said: "We have reached a decision. We have found the defendant guilty of murder in the first degree." Presently the judge stood up to render his sentence upon the prisoner. He said: "I sentence this young man to hang by the neck until he is dead." There was a hush over the courtroom. In the middle of the building an old man pushed his way out into the aisle, and came down to the front of the courtroom, put his hand on the judge's stand and looked into the face of the old judge who had just rendered the statement with reference to his son, and said: "Judge, I am an old man. This boy is the child of my old age. I realize that maybe I have made the mistake for which he is suffering the penalty. But, Judge, I will tell you what I want to do. I wish you would let me take his place on the scaffold; let me have the noose adjusted about my neck; let me stand on the trap door; let me drop into eternity for my child!" The judge looked at the old man for a moment, and then he said: "Old man, I am sorry that things are like this, but there isn't anything that I can do about it." Slowly the judge opened the pages of the big book before him and began to read. He said: "Let me read for you the laws of the state of Massachusetts:

'Every man shall, for his own crime, suffer the conse-
quences thereof himself.' You can't take his place. He
must bear his own burden in this life; he is responsible,
and while you may too be responsible, he is going to have
to bear his own responsibility." Where did that come
from? I'll tell you. It came from this Book (holding the
Bible). It was Paul who said: "Every knee shall bow to
me, and every tongue shall confess to God." But he said
also: "But everyone of us shall give account of himself to
God."

That is the way it is, brother. You are responsible, and
you must find out the truth, obey and live by it. You had
better make certain that you do not let something slip up
on you. You had better be sure that you are not allowing
something to get in the way, because one day you are going
to be held responsible for that which you have done while
you live on this earth.

Are you here tonight out of Christ? Then if you are,
why don't you make it right with Him tonight? Why don't
you do His bidding, come to the Lord, do His will, obey
His gospel? Are you out of duty? Get back into the
activities of the church again. Come back to your first
love, do the Lord's will once more and God will give you a
home when life is over. If you are a subject of the invitation, I beg you to come while together we stand and sing.

PICKUP: (After invitation song). I want to say to
you that I do appreciate the way that you have listened.
It is an inspiration to anyone to speak to people who listen
so well, and I want you to know that I am grateful for the
kindness along this line. I pray that God's blessings will
be upon you. You ponder the things that have been presented in this meeting and I trust that God will use those
things to His honor and glory, to my good and to your
good as we live here in this earth. May the Lord bless you
in every good thing:

PHILLIPS: You have made your own decision in this
service tonight, as well as in this series of meetings. I

stated on the opening night of these services that in my judgment and opinion I do not know anyone more capable to proclaim the gospel of Christ in an effective manner than Harry Pickup. I love him for his work's sake, and I am sure that if you had not known him until this series of meetings, you cannot help but be impressed by his convictions, by the earnestness in which he presented these lessons and by the soundness of every one of them. I do not know of a single thing presented that has not been in perfect harmony with God's will. It has been presented in such a fine manner: in the spirit of love for the lost and dying souls of men, and having the full assurance of conviction even in his expressions that someday he must give an account in the judgment. I cannot help but love him dearly.

If we should never meet again on this earth, impressions have been made in this service tonight and in the services that have gone before that will long live. Let us not forget the things we have learned in this meeting, but let us grow taller and stronger by applying whatever is lacking in our lives.

I want to say one word in connection with that which he said in the beginning of the service tonight. I had not thought too much about it until he mentioned it tonight. It concerns the absence of my father. Of course, at the time of the accident in which my father was killed, I did not think much about other matters. I felt the loss very keenly, perhaps more so than many others; it was a great loss to us all. Shortly after the accident I received many cards, telegrams and letters from many parts of the country expressing sympathy in our loss. But there was one letter that I got and read it not once or twice, but a dozen times or more. This letter was written on a piece of paper in long hand with a pencil, and it was signed at the bottom: Harry Pickup. That letter gave us much consolation because we knew of the great love Harry had for my father, and the love my father had for him. I know my father would have been here for every service if it had been possible—he was one of the elders here—but as he has "put off this tabernacle," we are thankful to a Loving Father for the pleasant memories in the associations of the past. Many such memories make impressions upon us that are lasting.

I want to make a few statements of gratitude and appreciation for those who have had some part in this meeting. Ordinarily they are not even noticed. We don't pay much attention to those who do little things that contribute so much to the success of a meeting. As an example: the flowers that have been so neatly arranged and carefully prepared each evening. Sister Emmette Jackson has been very faithful in doing that, not only in this meeting, but all the time. Sometimes I think we fall short in our responsibilitity and duty in not expressing things of that kind. We appreciate all those who have contributed in one way or another; in bringing people here who would not have come had it not been for them. Of course, we are grateful for the direction of the singing by Brother Cope, and in the fine and encouraging manner in which you sang. We are grateful for the encouragement of the neighboring congregations who have been so faithful to come each night. We are also grateful to those who came from this community, who are not members of the church of Christ. You are invited to attend every service at this place. If there is nothing else, let us pray.

CHRISTIAN EDUCATION: THE CHURCH

Due to a rather constant and consistent program of orientation on the subject, many people have either consciously or unconsciously connected the subject of Christian Education with but one thing: a school or college operated by members of the church where the Bible is daily taught to young people who are, at the same time, obtaining their academic education. The fact of the matter is (and we all know it, though we may have forgotten it) the church which Jesus built has as its primary function the responsibility of educating people to be Christians, hence CHRISTIAN EDUCATION.

The commission which Jesus announced to His apostles in Matthew 28:16-20, involved them in the responsibility of going out and teaching men the gospel of Christ, and then also teaching them all of the other things necessary to the carrying on of the work of the Lord, which Jesus proposed to bring to the remembrance of the apostles. If the evangelization of the world was to be accomplished by the teaching and preaching of these representatives of Jesus as they educated men in the doctrines of the faith, then here is an example of how the job is to be done which all posterity can follow.

Peter, one of the apostles of Jesus, evidently thought that was the idea when he delivered his Holy Spirit-guided discourse on the day the church was established, as we learn in the second chapter of Acts. He had been brought up at the feet of the Great Teacher, and on this memorable Pentecost he delivered a masterful sermon which was calculated to educate, even these crucifiers of Jesus, in the Christian principles of salvation. Quite a number of them "received" a rather elaborate education on the subject, according to Acts 2:41, for 3000 souls were added to the church.

But this was just the beginning: the church had the responsibility of continuing in the apostles doctrine and fellowship and the breaking of bread and in prayers, and someone had to teach them—educate them—how all this was to be done. The apostles, who took the lead in this, were certainly qualified, hence they doubtless assumed the major part of this work of indoctrination in the infant church. As they continued to preach the gospel others fell under the spell of their community educational program, for after Peter's sermon recorded in Acts 3, we learn that the number of church members had grown to 5000 (Acts 4:4)

The responsibility of the young church in Jerusalem was far greater than we can imagine. Thousands had to be taught how to worship scripturally as Christians, and had to be indoctrinated in their own responsibility as a part of the church of Christ. Their education as Christians included some rather drastic lessons in church discipline, as we learn upon reading the case of Ananias and Sapphira in Acts 5. But the instruction was effective. Great fear came upon the church and all others who heard about the incident, and it wasn't long until "multitudes both of men and women" were added to the church.

Just how effective CHRISTIAN EDUCATION actually was in the early church, is demonstrated in the lives of the ones who had received the training. Not many months passed before the leaders of Judaism came to the conclusion that they couldn't stamp out this new doctrine which had filled Jerusalem as easily as they had thought at first. They tried a program of counter teaching to offset the work carried on by the church. Examples of how they failed in these efforts are found in Acts 4:5-22, 5:34-42; 6:10.

So they turned to physical violence in earnest. Up to Acts 7 they had only used this as a sort of side line, more or less threateningly. Now they got down to business. They stoned Stephen to death, they scattered the disciples by driving them out of Jerusalem into the regions of Judea and Samaria, and Saul began his relentless persecution against the church by going into the homes of church-members, hauling them out and having them committed to prison.

This was a real testing of their faith in Christ and was the real proof of the effectiveness of their Christian training. The answer is found in Acts 8:4: "They that were scattered abroad went every where preaching the word." These disciples of the Lord were fully indoctrinated in the principles of New Testament Christianity. The church had done a thorough work in its part of the job in educating men out of Judaism into Christianity, and in educating them to be strong in faith and teaching. Jesus Christ Himself had taught their teachers that those who were taught of God, and who heard and learned the teaching would come to him, (John 6:45). This Jerusalem church —scattered to the four winds by a ruthless persecution— gave a very good account of themselves as both students and teachers, in God's great educational institution, the church for which Jesus died.

One of the things Paul admonished the church at Rome to do, as he wrote many general instructions in chapter 12, was to teach, exhort, prophesy. Numerous passages to the churches at Corinth, Galatia, Colosse, Ephesus and to the evangelists Timothy and Titus charge the congregations with the responsibility for continuing the educational program of divine instruction to both saint and sinner. The work of the church of Christ is that of CHRISTIAN EDUCATION: teaching men and women, boys and girls to be Christians and to live faithfully unto death.

CHRISTIAN EDUCATION: THE HOME

In spite of the fact that the home is the oldest type of group activity, some men have ceased to think of it as having any educational significance. Institutionalism, in the popular connection of the word has, at times, become such a vital factor in the pattern of men's lives that a few have lost sight of some of the real purposes for which God intended the home. Certainly one of the responsibilities which attaches itself to the home is the obligation to educate the members of the family.

One good example of this is a compliment paid to Abraham by God. The Lord said, "For I know him, that he will command his children and his household after him, and they shall keep the way of the Lord to do justice and judgment: that the Lord may bring upon Abraham that which he hath spoken of him." (Gen. 18:19).

Where did God expect Abraham to "command his children and his household" in order for them to know how to "keep the way of the Lord?" It was a home responsibility. Abraham had moved about quite a lot through the years, remaining in one locality but a comparatively short time. But whether he remained a long or a short time in one place, he had the responsibility of training his family in the "way of the Lord."

The patriarchal system emphasized this: It is quite likely that *all* training was done in the home because there were few, if any, outside means of obtaining this training. But whether there were or were not public facilities for supplementing certain phases of education, the responsibility was on the home.

During the time of Moses we find an injunction from God respecting the home as a fundamental educational organization. God said, "And these words which I command thee this day, shall be in thine heart: and thou shalt teach them diligently unto thy children, and thou shalt talk of them when thou sittest in thine house, and when thou walkest in the way, and when thou liest down, and when thou risest up." (Deut. 6:5-7). God has always expected man to follow the instructions given in order to get the job done properly. If Abraham had *not* commanded his children after him, they likely would not have kept the "way of the Lord." If the Israelites had not followed the commandment quoted from the Law of Moses, children would have grown up in ignorance of God and with contempt for His way. One of the ten commandments involved respect for and obedience to parents, with the attendant blessings for keeping the instruction. God expected men to follow His law and indoctrinate their families. The general breakdown among the Jews, spiritually, after they came into Canaan, was due, in part at least, to the breakdown in home training concerning the things which would keep the family in the way of the Lord.

When Joshua gathered the twelve tribes together to give them his closing admonition, he urged them to put away false gods and serve Jehovah. Then he went a step further and told them that if they chose not to do this, that such conduct on their part would not effect his decision in the matter. In emphatic words he let it be known that he and his family intended to serve the Lord—even if they had to do it by themselves. (Josh. 24:14,15).

This great man of God evidently knew what he was talking about. He always had on other occasions and there isn't anything here to indicate to the contrary. Even *one* can be a potent force in the community—if that home recognizes its responsibility in the field of spiritual education. It is quite possible that all the little people in Joshua's household had the benefit of the finest instruction there was to be obtained among the Israelites. It is a certain fact that a father who proposed to have *his* home travel the straight and narrow—even if the whole nation went spiritually beserk—already had set up a home training program that would make it unlikely that he might have to eat his words.

Principles are eternal, hence the home as pictured in the New Testament differs not at all from the description given in the Old. With the change of the covenant there would be, of necessity, a change in what the parents taught the children or others in the home, but the home itself occupies the same relationship to education per see that it held from the beginning.

Paul gives specific instructions to both parents and children in Ephesians 6:1-4 as he quotes one of the basic lessons on home training from the Law of Moses. Children are to be "brought up" in the home; this "bringing up" is to be "in the nurture and admonition of the Lord."

This is, perhaps, one of the most comprehensive scriptures in the Bible. It embraces everything that constitutes a child's upbringing. All commandments and instructions given to all classes of people concerning all that God wants them to know should, fittingly, be taught from the pulpit, in the classroom *and* in the home. There are some subjects, however, that are undoubtedly more suited to home instruction because of their intimate nature. Specific education of young Christian women by older Christian women, for example (Tit. 2:1-5) in more appropriately conducted in the home relationship or women's classes. The widow's children mentioned in I Timothy 5:4 are to learn—before anything else—to show piety or respect at home.

This is all CHRISTIAN EDUCATION even though quietly carried on within the four walls of an humble Christian home without any fanfare from an elaborate public relations department of a school or college—or even a high-pressure "special program" of the local church.

CHRISTIAN EDUCATION—THE SCHOOL

"I am no match for my unbelieving professors in the University. They are wrecking my faith in God and the Bible." These were the words of a fine young man who had been a student in that institution for about six months. That same year 23 other students filled out registration blanks indicating that they were either members of the church of Christ, or gave this as their preference. Most of these young men attended the services at the local congregation at the beginning of the first semester. By the end of the second semester all but four had succumbed to either the lure of the world, indifference or perhaps to the same "unbelieving professors" who "wrecked the faith" of the first young man. A Christian father stood on the campus of Florida Christian College and, with tears running down his cheeks, told of two stalwart sons—once faithful to Christ—who were lost through the influence of unbelieving instructors who had no respect for God, Christ or the Bible.

Examples of such could be multiplied, but these are sufficient to show that the responsibility of parents extend beyond the Christian education to which their children are exposed in the home and in the church. Secular education is a parental responsibility along with the many other obligations which are so much a part of the business of training a child in the way he should go. Many mothers and fathers who carefully teach their children in the *home*, and who see to it that they have regular and consistent training and instruction at the public services of the *church*, have permitted their faith in the purity of the "little red schoolhouse" to lead them to believe that all educational organizations are just as devoted to the faith of their children as are they. Obviously this is not true.

Boys and girls are going home from public school classes in Biology pointing out to startled mothers and fathers that the Genesis account of creation is not necessarily true, that God made men by the process of organic evolution and that a whale's throat is too small to swallow a man, hence the story of Jonah is unscientific!

God has charged parents with the responsibilitity of seeing to it that such faith-wrecking foolishness, which is founded upon human opinions and unfounded assumptions, is not crammed down the throats of our boys and girls. Specific instructions are given to fathers to nurture their offspring in the "chastening and admonition of the Lord." (Eph. 6:4)

Some comment here on the two words translated "chastening" and "admonition" will possibly clarify matters some. Few parents realize the significance of these two expressions. For example the word which we translate "chastening" comes from "paideia" concerning which Thayer says:

> "The whole training and education of children (which relates to the cultivation of mind and morals, and employs for this purpose now commands and admonitions, now reproof and punishment) ; Eph. 6:4."

An additional statement given in parenthesis by Mr. Thayer states that in the Greek written from the days of Aeschylus (which would be about 525 B.C.) the word "includes also the care and training of the body."

Thayer says in defining the word we translate "admonition" which comes from the Greek "nouthesia":

"Admonition, exhortation Sap. 16:6; I Cor. 10:11; Tit. 3:10; kurion, such as belongs to the Lord (Christ) or proceeds from him, Eph. 6:4."

Thus we learn that the Holy Spirit did not intend for parents to subject their children to *any* kind of education that would mitigate His instructions that the "whole training and education of children" be according to "such as belongs to the Lord (Christ) or proceeds from him." Parents who willfully or unwittingly place their children under the influence of instruction which destroys faith— hence which definitely *does not* proceed from the Lord— and who make little or no effort to offset such or correct it, are not only violating Paul's divine injunction but may live to reap, in sorrow, the fruits of their failure.

If the reader makes an application of the foregoing to the effect that he assumes that the writer intended the conclusion to be drawn that the safest place for a child to be educated is in a school or college operated by faithful members of the New Testament church, then the writer is happy; this is exactly the point intended!

God has laid upon Christian fathers and mothers the responsibility of *all* their training both spiritual and academic. Obviously much of this training is given by others than the parents of the child, men and women who are academically fitted to impart the sciences, language, history, etc. But the parent still holds his position of responsibility relative to the faith of the child. He might not be fully acquainted with all the ramifications connected with the theory of organic evolution, but it doesn't require a masters degree in Physical Science for the parent to know that some changes need to be made when little

Johnny comes home with the fantastic tales (tails) told him by his biology teacher.

Many people have either consciously or unconsciously connected the subject of Christian Education with but one thing: Bible instruction given in a school or college operated by members of the church. Many more have either consciously or inconsciously connected Christian Education with the instructions received at home from parents or at church from the Sunday school teacher or the preacher's sermon. Neither of these positions is correct. Home training is the art of being a faithful Christian—given at home—is of vast importance, but it is not enough. The instruction services of the church are indispensible, but the responsibility of the parents goes even beyond taking the child to three or four of these each week. The parent must see to it that the instruction he receives *outside* the home and *away* from the church building does not upset the plan of God for the child's "whole training and education" to be "such as belongs to the Lord (Christ) or proceeds from him."

GIVING: SOME THINGS GOD SAYS

Many Christians are still squirmish about sermons on giving, even though the New Testament has more to say about this subject—with warnings against violations of the divine instructions concerning it—than the subject of baptism. The first sin-scandal within the church soon after the day of Pentecost, was connected with the financial program. Ananias and Sapphira, as recorded in the fifth chapter of Acts, did three things:

1. They AGREED together about their attempted deception;
2. They KEPT BACK part of what they proposed to give (they said they gave it "all");
3. They BOTH LIED after they were caught.

Failure to carry on a scriptural program of church finance can become the downfall of an otherwise scriptural congregation. This is true not only because that the few who carry the greater part of the financial burden of the church may become discouraged in time, but it is also true because of a wrong attitude toward the Lord's work which can result in a spiritual breakdown.

There are a number of PRINCIPLES which govern this question which I am discussing, and I conscientiously believe that no member of the church can do his full duty in respect to his worship until and unless he understands and applies these principles. I shall discuss them under the several headings which follow and shall give the scripture which I believe teaches the principle.

1. JESUS TEACHES THAT GIVING IS A MATTER OF FAITHFULNESS OR UNFAITHFULNESS IN THE MATTER OF STEWARDSHIP.

Luke 16:10-12: "He that is faithful in that which is least is faithful also in much: and he that is unjust in the least is unjust also in much. If therefore ye have not been faithful in the unrighteous mammon (money), who will commit to your trust the true riches? And if you have not been faithful in that which is another man's, who shall give you that which is your own?"

It is very plain to see in this that Jesus regards all the property and money which we have in this world as belonging to God, and that God regards us as STEWARDS who are only given custody of this property and money for a limited time. Jesus shows in this parable that this property is NOT OURS—it belongs to another, God. The point is that if we don't know how to USE what God has given to us—as stewards—then he will NOT give us the eternal inheritance which should be ours. What God lets you earn, the money you receive for your work and the house you purchase with the fruits of your labors, are GOD'S, not yours. What He proposes to give to us hereafter, is OURS. If we can't take care of HIS by the proper use of it, then He will not give us OURS.

You can see from this principle that you can spend this money which God lets you earn, on yourself and family—if you choose to do so—and not use the proper amount of it for the Lord's work, just as you please. *But such unfaithfulness in stewardship will rob you of your eternal reward.* In brief, my brother, it is give, as God has prospered you or be damned! I realize that's strong language, but it is the teaching of Jesus on the matter of stewardship of money and possessions.

2. Another principle, in the matter of church finances, is: GOD EXPECTS US TO GIVE—AND ORDERS US TO GIVE—AS THE LORD HAS PROSPERED US.

I Cor. 16:1,2: "Now concerning the collection for the saints, as I have given order to the churches of Galatia, even so do ye. Upon the first day of the week let every one of you lay by him in store, as God hath prospered him, that there be no gatherings when I come."

Please note that the word "order" is used. The English word here is translated from the Greek word "diatasso" which is a strong word that actually prescribes limits. The dictionary says that the word means: "to give commands, to prescribe." The word appears in the work of Jesus when he "directed" (dietaksen) the people to give to a child which He had healed, something to ear (Luke 8:55). According to Paul's reference to the matter, the Lord did "order" (dietaksen) the ones who preach the gospel to live of the gospel. The speech which Jesus made to His disciples in the 10th chapter of Matthew, when he sent out the twelve on the limited commission, is referred to by Matthew as the Lord's "commanding" (diatassown) them (Matt. 11:1). Paul said the Lord's coming had been "ordained" (Dietageis) (Gal. 3:19).

There are more than a half dozen other examples which I could give all of which show that what Paul said about the first day of the week collection—or contribution—was an ORDER, a COMMAND.

Well, most people accept that: they believe to contribute of their means on the first day of the week (as stated in I Cor. 16:1,2) is a command. I am not only making this point—for I believe you accept the fact that we should contribute on that day; the point I am making is that *the Lord has ordered you to give as you have been prospered!* We are great believers in the fact that Sunday is the TIME to give, all right; where we fall down is that the order also extends to the AMOUNT we give. God ordered that too.

I am not prepared to state, today or at any other time, that I can—by faith, which comes from hearing God's Word—say that the scriptures teach in so many words what that exact amount is. What I am going to say is that the Holy Spirit has ORDERED YOU to give as you have been prospered.

I read the following recently:

"He does not mean to suggest any proportion by his law, As God hath prospered him. Readily he means, Let your separation for others be according to your sense of God's goodness to you."

Allow me to commend this statement to you. The ORDER, therefore, not only to the church at Corinth, but also to the church at any place, is that each member give on the first day of the week according to his sense of God's goodness to him.

3. A third principle which I would like to present on finances is: GOD'S SYSTEM OF GIVING IS ONE OF EQUALITY.

2 Cor. 8-11-14: "Now therefore perform the doing of it (referring to their contribution for the poor saints) that as there was a readiness to will, so there may be a performance also out of that which ye have. For if there be first a willing mind it is accepted according to that a man hath, and not according to that he hath not. For I mean not that other men be eased, and ye burdened; but by an equality, that now at this time your abundance may be a supply for their want, that their abundance also may be a supply for your want: that there may be equality."

We accept this principle in all other walks of life. In our social contacts with others, we believe and practice the principle of equality. Each person pays his or her share of any social event that involves the action of the group, and no man would hesitate about giving his share, because it is one of those self-evident moral principles that all human beings acknowledge at once. There is equality: those who are better able to give than others give more (as they are prospered, so to speak), and those who have smaller incomes give less (likewise, as they are prospered). This principle, with regard to church finance, is just as scriptural as dropping your money in the contribution on the "first day of the week."

I do not think I should have very much respect for myself if I had to carry around in my soul the humiliating conviction that I was giving less, in proportion to my ability to support the financial needs of the church, than the other members. But how is the proportion to be determined? The answer comes back, of course, "Let every one of you lay by him in store as God hath prospered him," and that's right. The rub comes when each of us decides what would be right according to what we receive.

If I am left to determine this by myself, I may be apt to under-estimate what is my proportion—based upon my income. My own selfishness might also prompt me to overestimate what you ought to give as your proportion. How then, can we settle this matter? Why friends, it is perfectly obvious that such could be easily left to somebody who is entirely disinterested in the matter. This should be somebody who can help me decide the matter without being biased by selfishness—who can look at me, and at that other brother, and make a fair disinterested estimate of the relative ability of each.

Well, it just so happens that God has someone in His church who would be perfectly unbiased, unprejudiced and very fair in this—or any other matter. In fact, some of the reasons for appointing them to the office they hold in the church are that they are "vigilant, sober, not greedy of filthy lucre or gain, not covetous, patient, apt to teach" (hence they know what the Book teaches) and on top of all this they are "not a novice" hence they have had lots of experience. Obviously, I refer to the elders of the church. One of the jobs of the elders is to watch for our souls, hence they could certainly be depended upon to tell us just what amount we should scripturally give out of what income we have.

So far as I know there has never been anyone to object to the duty of the elders to "watch" for the souls of the members, but when it comes to having anyone to counsel with the members on how much they ought to give, there are a lot of people who say that "My contribution is nobody's business but mine and God's." There is a sense in which this is true. There is a sense in which ALL of your conduct is nobody's business but yours and God's; but there is another sense in which this is absolutely NOT true.

For instance: idleness and gossiping is not only the business of the guilty Christian and God; it is likewise the business of the elders and the church. Paul states that such a one should have the fellowship of the church withdrawn from him, and the reference is 2 Thess. 3:6-12.

In I Cor. 5:6-13 Paul tells the church to purge itself of any person—who is a brother—guilty of a long list of sins. Listed in this group is the covetous man. Is covetousness nobody's business but the covetor's and God's? No, it is the business of the church as well. If there is a possibility that one slip into ANY of these sins—and certainly in the matter of money there is a great danger —why wouldn't it be right for the elders to assist the members in deciding what is proper? Why should these bishops of God's flock be held accountable by God for dealing with all the sins in the catalogue of which members may be guilty—and help them to avoid them, and yet not be required to assist the members in this?

As I read through the New Testament, I find that the sin of covetousness or stinginess, is more frequently held up to condemnation by the Lord and the apostles, and dealt with in severer and more terrific terms, than any other sin in the whole category. Indeed, a covetous man is more unlike Christ than any other wicked man in the world. A drunkard, may—and often does—have a good deal of kindness and good-heartedness about him. A man who kills another in a heat of passion may—in many ways —be a good kind person; but if a man is covetous, stingy, penurius, miserly with God, he is farther away from Christ and His aptitude toward things, than all the rest. Jesus gave up Heaven and came down to earth to live. While on earth he gave up all of the things that ordinary mortals consider desirable, and finally gave His life for the benefit of others. But the covetous man, this poor wretch who wants everything for himself—except a small pittance which he drops in the contribution basket to salve his conscience—is actualy not giving anything. Not only is he unfaithful in the matter of stewardship, having forgotten that the money is not his at all, he has a very poor conception of God's goodness to him, in the matter of his prosperity, and has absolutely no regard for God's commands relative to equality.

4. The fourth principle which I want to discuss with you, my brethren, is that GOD'S SYSTEM REQUIRES CHEERFUL GIVING.

2 Cor. 9:6,7: "But this I say, He which soweth sparingly shall reap also sparingly; and he which soweth bountifully shall reap also bountifully. Every man accordingly as he purposeth in his heart, so let him give; not grudgingly, or of necessity; for God loveth a cheerful giver."

I doubt if a passage of scripture in the New Testament is abused more than this passage—unless it be the one I discussed in the second heading of this lesson. Cheerfulness must grace all the giving done by Christians, in order for it to be acceptable to the Lord. The Lord DOES NOT love a grudging giver, and God also DOES NOT love a stingy person. Some people seem to think they can escape the judgment of God by saying to themselves that they can't give cheerfully (what they really ought to give) so they will give a little and be cheerful.

Don't think you can escape the judgment of God by doing it that way. It is true that God doesn't want your contribution if it is given "grudgingly," but God doesn't want YOU—even though you may be a very cheerful little person about the pittance you give to Him—unless you give according to your prosperity. The part of the passage that condemns this fellow is the first: "He which soweth sparingly shall reap also sparingly."

9 781584 271635